UNDESIRABLES

Tell us what you
think of this book.

**READ IT AND VISIT
WWW.UNDESIRABLES.CA
BY FEBRUARY 15, 2012**

You could win
a prize package of
Ali Kazimi's films.

ALI KAZIMI

UNDESIRABLES

WHITE CANADA AND THE KOMAGATA MARU

AN ILLUSTRATED HISTORY

Douglas & McIntyre
D&M PUBLISHERS INC.
Vancouver/Toronto/Berkeley

This book was made possible through the generous
support of the Community Historical Recognition
Program of Citizenship and Immigration Canada.

 Citizenship and   Citoyenneté et
Immigration Canada   Immigration Canada

Douglas & McIntyre
An imprint of D&M Publishers Inc.
2323 Quebec Street, Suite 201
Vancouver BC Canada V5T 4S7
www.douglas-mcintyre.com

Cataloguing data available from Library
and Archives Canada
ISBN 978-1-55365-653-1 (cloth)

Editing by Barbara Pulling
Copyediting by Pam Robertson
Jacket and interior design by Jessica Sullivan
Front jacket photographs: *top:* Leonard Frank
photograph, Vancouver Public Library, VPL 6226;
bottom: Vancouver Public Library—Special
Collections, VPL 6227
Back jacket photographs: *top:* Leonard Frank
photograph, Vancouver Public Library, VPL 6231;
bottom: City of Vancouver Archives, CVA 7-126
Printed and bound in China by C&C Offset
Printing Co., Ltd.
Text printed on acid-free paper

Douglas & McIntyre gratefully acknowledges the
financial support of the Canada Council for the Arts,
the British Columbia Arts Council, the Province of
British Columbia through the Book Publishing Tax
Credit and the Government of Canada through the
Canada Book Fund for its publishing activities.

PAGE II Officers of the Fifty-third Sikh (Frontier Force)
Regiment, 1911.

PAGE III The king of Canada & the king-emperor of India,
Kaiser-e-Hind George V, portrayed as the colonel-in-chief of
the Tiwana Lancers (Eighteenth King George's Own Lancers)
of the British Indian Army, 1922.

PAGE IV European immigrants on the deck of a ship taking
them to Canada. In 1913, Canada accepted over 400,000
immigrants of European descent, while Asian immigrants
were restricted and virtually shut out through a variety of
means.

PAGE V Passengers aboard the *Komagata Maru* were
subjected to deliberate delays in processing, along with the
withholding of food and water.

PAGE VI In July 1914, passengers line the rail of the *Komagata
Maru* as an immigration boat carrying Canadian officials and
military officers sits alongside.

PAGE VII Prime Minister Robert Borden built upon the
immigration policies of his predecessors. Like them, he
imagined Canada as a "white man's country."

PAGE VIII British Indian postage stamps with busts of British
monarchs—Queen Victoria, Edward VII and George V.

PAGE IX This 1898 stamp features a line from Lewis Morris's
poem "A Song of Empire": "We hold a vaster Empire than has
been! / Nigh half the race of man is subject to our Queen! /
Nigh half the wide, wide Earth is ours in fee! / And where her
rule comes, all are free."

DEDICATED TO ALL THOSE WHO
STRUGGLED FOR EQUALITY IN CANADA,
AND TO THOSE WHO COULD NOT LAND

CONTENTS

———

PREFACE AND
ACKNOWLEDGEMENTS

PEOPLE HAVE WONDERED why I wanted to tell the story of the *Komagata Maru*. "It is a Sikh story," they say, "and you are Muslim, aren't you?" I tell them, "I grew up in Delhi believing in the ideal of a secular, democratic India." Having lived more than half my life in Canada, I am committed to the idea of building a pluralistic, inclusive and just society here.

Even though I did not have relatives aboard the *Komagata Maru*, the story has become a part of my life. I spent eight years making a documentary film about the *Komagata Maru* called *Continuous Journey.* The film gave me the opportunity to shed some light on this so-called "dark chapter" in Canada's history. Researching the history helped me to find my place in the Canadian landscape and to feel at home on Canadian soil. I see the turning away of the *Komagata Maru* in 1914 as a transformative moment not just for Canada but also for British India and the British Empire.

Rarely does one get a chance to reframe a project for another medium. Ventures like these are not possible without significant support—and central to this project is my wife and partner, Heidi McKenzie, without whose initiative and determination this book would not exist. I am indebted to a multitude of people: Ena Dua, Hugh Johnston, Audrey Macklin and Ramdeo Sampat-Mehta, whose groundbreaking research and writings on this subject have become central to anyone working on early South Asian history in Canada; Zulfikar Hirji, for his generous and incisive

THE HINDUSTANEE

The Official Organ of the United India League

Volume I	Vancouver, B. C., Sunday, March 1, 1914	Number III.

Shreematee Beebee Harnamkor, the beloved wife of Bai Bhag Singh, the president of the Khalsa Dewan Society, died at her home in Fairview, on the 30th of January, 1914, at 6 p. m., at the early age of 28. She leaves, besides her husband, Bhai Bhag Singh, to mourn her memory, two young children. The elder, Jopindra, is 26 months old, while her baby daughter was only 9 days old when left motherless.

The whole Hindu colony of British Columbia was thrown into grief over the untimely and unexpected death of this highly respected Sikh lady in Vancouver.

She was the inspiration of the whole community of Sikhs and Hindustanees, by her kind, courteous and patronizing qualities, and was the leading woman amongst the few Sikh ladies who have landed on these shores, who are deeply grieved over her loss.

The "Agni Sanskar" funeral took place in the enclosure reserved at the cemetery for the Hindu colony, and the occasion was a very mournful one, when the largest number of mourners ever seen at a Hindustanee funeral in Vancouver were deeply moved with sorrow at the sight of the funeral pyre

SHREEMATEE BEEBEE HARNAMKOR
Deceased Wife of Bhai Bhag Singh, Born 1886; Died 1914.

which reduced the lifeless body of this honored lady into five elementals.

Granthi Bhai Hari Singh read the the service as per Sikh rites, so that her spirit rests in eternal happiness.

Her husband, Bhai Bhag Singh, communicated to the mourners the charities willed by the deceased lady, which he stated will be duly executed.

She was born at Peshawar, a country which resembles British Columbia in scenery and climate.

Up to the time of the birth of her baby daughter and a few days after, she was in perfect health, but obstetric trouble unexpectedly occurred, which proved fatal in spite of all the best medical services obtainable.

This was the same family which the Immigration Authorities had ordered deported and was placed in their custody at the immigration shed until the habeas corpus proceeding brought their release.

It was not possible to imagine that the cruel hand of death would claim this distinguished Sikh lady as its victim within 24 months of her entering Vancouver, B. C.

We herein record our deep sorrow for the bereavement suffered by the Bhai Bhag Singh family.

review of the manuscript; Tasleem Thawar and Tim McCaskell, for reading and responding to drafts; Sadhu Binning; Pardeep Nagra; Sandeep Singh Brar; T. Sher Singh; Simmy Makhijani; Zaheed Mawani; Anna Withrow; Rana Chhina, childhood friend and brother-in-law, whose passion and excitement opened my eyes to hidden histories; Zool Suleman, whose friendship, courage and support continue to inspire me; Jack Uppal, Ratna Ghosh and Iqbal Gill for their endorsement of this project; Allison Urowitz, for putting us together with Douglas & McIntyre; editor Barbara Pulling, for her patience, diligence and gentle prodding; the late Ted Sibia and Kesar Singh, who were inspirational in their research and collection of early histories and materials on Punjabi migrants to North America; Pam Robertson, for her copy editing; Jessica Sullivan, for her wonderful design; and Susan Meiselas, for visual inspiration. A special thanks to Library and Archives Canada, which remains an underappreciated national treasure; without it, this history would have been lost.

I am also indebted to the countless people, such as Edward Bird, whose refusal to be silenced in the face of intimidation and fear gives us sustenance in the ongoing protection of human rights, the rule of law and democratic freedoms.

My intent is to show that the *Komagata Maru* "incident" was not incidental in the context of Canada's desire to be a "white man's country." The full story of the ship's turning away demands an unflinching examination of both the past and the present. My hope is that this book will contribute to an evolving conversation about race and immigration in Canada.

OVERLEAF A photomontage created from two archival images, which was used as the publicity still for Ali Kazimi's award-winning feature documentary *Continuous Journey* (2004).

FAR LEFT The *Hindustanee* was one of a handful of early magazines filled with community news and funded by advertisements for small businesses. Published in English from 1913 to 1914 by the United India League, it sought to bridge the divide between South Asians and Anglo-Canadians.

LEFT On July 23, 1914, after being anchored for two months in Vancouver's harbour, the *Komagata Maru* became the first ship carrying immigrants to be turned away from Canadian shores.

*"That Canada must remain a white man's country
is seen necessary on moral and political grounds."*
WILLIAM LYON MACKENZIE KING quoting British
authorities in his report on his mission to England, 1908[1]

INTRODUCTION

"THE *KOMAGATA MARU* was mentioned in our history textbook," insists an old school friend from Delhi. He remembers the book clearly, but I don't. Although I was fascinated by the layers upon layers of ruins that surrounded us in New Delhi in the 1970s, I was bored stiff by the way history was taught: an endless chronology of dynastic periods, kings, battles and dates that had to be memorized for the dreaded final exams. Our textbooks conveyed none of the magic and mystery that shrouded the past.

I started engaging with history as a collector instead. I had inherited my grandfather's stamp collection, and I found a kindred spirit in Rana Chhina, who was a year senior to me at school. We were soon absorbed in deciphering the chronology of the recent monarchs of the British Empire, from Victoria to George VI, whose busts appeared with striking monotony on the stamps of British India. Gradually, our interest spread to colonial coins, which we bought from transient vendors at the kabadi bazar. Every Sunday we'd make the long bus journey from South Delhi to the outskirts of the city, along the eastern ramparts of the seventeenth-century Red Fort built by the Mughals. Among the coins we came across was the occasional military medal, and Rana became increasingly interested in these. We'd huddle together in the British Council Library, checking in the catalogues to identify what we'd gathered.

Rana's family was Sikh, with deep roots in the Punjab. I came from a Muslim family rooted in different parts of India, Bihar in the east and Hyderabad in the south. My parents had had an arranged marriage, because my grandfathers had become good friends during their time at Cambridge in the mid-1920s. My family moved to Delhi when I was four, and we lived in predominantly Punjabi neighbourhoods. In spite of Rana's unshorn hair and turban, he, like me, grew up in the secular milieu of English-speaking, middle-class India.

Rana's paternal grandfather had served in the British Indian Army in the Fifty-third Sikh Regiment—troops celebrated by colonial writers such as Rudyard Kipling as the renowned "Frontier Force." Rana was the proud owner of his grandfather's military uniform, medals and papers and a group of his military photographs. As time passed, Rana immersed himself more deeply in the historical world of the British Indian Army. I was along for the ride, engrossed in the thrill of finding medals that alluded to forgotten battles.

The British Indian Army remains an enigma in modern Indian history, and arguably in the Indian psyche. The force was used not only to subjugate the rebellious parts of British India but also to extend the British Empire's reach in Asia and Africa. Despite the mountains of popular books that continue to be published about the First and Second World Wars, few people know that the British Indian Army played a key role in both conflicts. In fact, it was the largest volunteer army in both world wars.

There are some memorials that recognize the Indian Army's contribution. When the British designed New Delhi, they built the India Gate, a magnificent memorial to the 90,000 Indian soldiers who died in the Anglo-Afghan Wars and the First World War. As a child, I visited the monument with my father, who pointed out the names carved along its sides. He never explained whom these men had been fighting or why they had died.

The India Gate stands at one end of an impressive avenue originally called the King's Way and known today as the Rajpath. At the opposite end of the avenue is the Presidential Palace, the Rashtrapati Bhavan, with its two symmetrical edifices, the North and South Blocks. Every year on January 26, Republic Day, an impressive military parade starts in front of this former viceregal palace in New Delhi, winding through a frigid winter fog down Raisina Hill, along Rajpath, and past the India Gate to end up at the Red Fort. The majority of the regiments, in their ceremonial uniforms, battle colours and standards, reference the British Indian Army's record in Asia, Africa and Europe. Most people watching the spectacle fail to appreciate the paradox of a parade that celebrates simultaneously India's colonial military history, its nationalism and its military aspirations.

Sikhs formed 1.5 per cent of the population of British India, but they made up 25 per cent of the British Indian Army. Yet after 1914, as Sikh historians point out, no other community paid a higher price in the freedom struggle against the yoke of British colonialism. Between 1914 and 1947, ninety-three Sikh men were hanged, and more than two thousand were sentenced to life imprisonment in the Andaman Islands.[2] What happened? How did such unrelenting opposition emerge?

Rana's parents often hosted old friends from Punjab. A Sikh couple, Prem Singh and Dalbir Kaur, had apparently been members of the Communist Party. Dalbir Aunty's father and grandfather had been cavalrymen in the British Indian Army. More remarkably, her uncle had been a passenger on the *Komagata Maru* and had belonged to the Ghadar Party. Organizing in North America, the Ghadarites were involved in a short-lived armed struggle against the British between 1914 and 1917. Over dinner I listened to the adults telling stories about bombings, years spent in hiding, conspiracy cases and hangings. Their accounts presented a picture of the Indian fight to gain freedom from British colonialism radically different from that of Gandhi's near-mythic nonviolent struggle. Intriguing anecdotes about the Ghadarites were tucked away in my subconscious, and this hidden history would resurface years later during my excavations of the *Komagata Maru* incident.

I HAD NEVER dreamed of coming to Canada. From high school geography class I could roughly place the Great Lakes on a map and name them, and I knew where the Rockies were. At the Asia '72 fair in Delhi, in Canada's impressive modernist pavilion, I saw giant combines set against gigantic photo displays of endless wheat fields.

After graduating from the University of Delhi with a degree in science, I became interested in documentary filmmaking. In 1983, I was one of two students chosen for an exchange program with York University in Toronto. It was my first trip outside India, and the degree to which I had been acclimatized to English culture struck me when we landed at London's Heathrow Airport. The sense of familiarity was reassuring, yet deeply unsettling. I felt colonized.

OVERLEAF Gurmukh Singh Lalton, with niece Dalbir Kaur on his left, being greeted upon his release from prison in 1947 after India's declaration of independence. Radicalized by his experience as a seventeen-year-old passenger on the *Komagata Maru,* he had been serving a life sentence due to his activities as a Ghadar Party member.

LEFT The author *(left)* with his friend Rana Chhina at Rohtang Pass, India, 1979.

At the airport in Toronto, a uniformed officer asked my fellow student and me to step out of the immigration line. He examined our Indian passports and our Canadian student visas, then asked us to follow him to his office. In a bare room, across an empty desk, we were grilled for what seemed like an eternity. The officer was not sure our papers were in order, he said. How was he to know we had not bought them in some back street in Delhi? My friend and I vehemently denied doing any such thing. "Why don't you call our professor? He's waiting for us outside," we suggested. But the officer persisted. "Where is all the money this letter says you have for your scholarship? Which suitcase is it in?" We were shocked at this line of questioning and reiterated our position. The officer eventually stopped flipping through our passports, stamped them and handed them back. "The only reason I'm letting you into my country is because you speak such good English," he informed us. "You will always remember me," he added with a smile. Over the next six years, I encountered immigration officers whenever I went to renew my student visa and then when I applied for permanent residence in Canada. Some were kind, others officious. A few were like the one we had met on our arrival.

As I learned about Canada and Canadian history, questions started bubbling within me. If Canada was such a multicultural, tolerant and welcoming society, why were Canadians overwhelmingly of European descent? Why were second-generation, Canadian-born South Asian children inevitably asked, "Where are you from?" Why was the Indian diaspora overwhelmingly from the Punjab and made up mostly of people from Sikh backgrounds? One did not have to dig deep for dark chapters. I had arrived in the aftermath of a horrific period of so-called "Paki-bashing" that had crossed the Atlantic from the U.K. and swept across Canada in the 1970s. South Asians were not only shunned but subjected to racial taunts and slurs. All too often, these were accompanied by brutal physical violence, peaking in a man being pushed to his death in the path of an oncoming train in a Toronto subway station. To this day, I hear pain, anger, humiliation and sadness in the voices of friends who survived this period, as they acknowledge, "It was different then; those were really racist times." I faced some lingering after-effects in the early 1980s. I was deeply troubled by the casual "Paki" jokes that some still found acceptable, and a few times I was refused the rental of an apartment because I was South Asian. South Asians in Canada, even those who were clearly Canadian, remained "the other."

At the same time, I watched helplessly on television as India went through an upheaval of great proportions. The state of Punjab was wracked by violence. For decades, the demands of Sikhs, who formed about half the population of Punjab, had gone unheeded by the Indian government. By the early 1980s, Sikhs articulated feelings of disempowerment and marginalization, and their disenfranchisement gave rise to a separatist movement whose goal was to carve out a Sikh homeland called Khalistan. The government, led by Prime Minister Indira Gandhi, unleashed India's security forces to put down the separatists. Many members of the Sikh diaspora in Canada and all over the world supported the separatists.

In June 1984, the Indian Army was called in to surround the holiest shrine in Sikhism, Harmandir Sahib, the Golden Temple. The government of India claimed the temple had become the nerve centre for terrorism and housed hundreds of separatists. As the siege intensified, tensions escalated. The army did what to many was unthinkable: it launched a massive and bloody attack on the Golden Temple. The estimated number of those killed ranged from one to five thousand.[3]

These events resonated in Canada. Indian flags were burned in the streets of Toronto as many Canadian Sikhs reacted with rage. Four months later, Indira Gandhi's two trusted Sikh bodyguards gunned her down as she walked out to her garden for a television interview. While India went into shock, separatists handed out sweets in the streets of Vancouver and Toronto. Indira Gandhi's body had barely been cremated before Delhi was engulfed in flames and bloodshed. Indian human rights organizations laid bare the complicity among politicians, bureaucrats and the police that allowed the mobs seeking revenge to tear across Delhi. An estimated three thousand people were slaughtered.[4] The number could have been far greater if not for the courage of the many people who put their lives on the line to save others. My friend Rana had recently married my sister. Even though he was now an officer in the Indian Air Force, his family's safety was not guaranteed. I felt their pain and anguish halfway around the world.

In June 1985, Air India Flight 182 disintegrated in midair over the Irish Sea. My friends and I watched in shock as the first television images came in, showing shattered debris with the distinctive logo of the airline clearly visible. There were no survivors. Speaking to reporters, Canadian prime minister Brian Mulroney said he had conveyed his condolences to Indian prime minister Rajiv Gandhi. Upon hearing that, a white Canadian friend leaned over and said to me, "I am sorry, Ali." I exploded in fury, screaming at no one in particular: "They were Canadians, they were Canadians!" It would take twenty-five years and another Canadian prime minister to acknowledge that most of them "were our fellow citizens."[5] At the time, there was no national sense of mourning. For many Canadians, these were East Indians flying on an Indian aircraft, blown up by Sikh separatists motivated by events in India. Many Canadians felt little connection to the victims or the surviving families. I recognized the painful limbo inhabited by many Canadians of Indian origin. They had given up their Indian citizenship to legally become Canadians, yet in their darkest hour their adopted country had disowned them.

The following year, many Canadians convulsed with panic when a ship arrived off Newfoundland carrying Tamils fleeing the civil war in Sri Lanka. Similar hysteria ensued in 1987 when a shipload of Sikhs claiming refuge from political repression in Punjab arrived on the coast of Nova Scotia. The Canadian government's response to these refugees was frantic, particularly in the case of the Sikhs. Parliament was recalled from summer recess to deal with this national emergency, and a restrictive immigration bill was passed. There was much talk in the media about "queue-jumpers" and the need to control immigration. The government used coded phrases such as "due process" when addressing the issue of immigration. To be fair, Canadians had two opposing responses to the refugees. The sentiments in the vicious, racist opinion pieces published in newspapers were echoed by some citizens, but a few Canadian communities showed great kindness towards the new arrivals.

These events and the responses they generated made me uneasy about the relationship between race and national identity. I doubt very much Canada would have reacted in the same manner had a ship carrying white refugees from post-apartheid South Africa arrived on its shores.

In the spring of 1986, three years into film school, I got an opportunity to edit a documentary film in Vancouver. Vancouver was reputed to be almost as diverse a city as Toronto; I found it a disquietingly segregated place. The downtown and its immediate neighbourhoods were overwhelmingly white. Chinatown and the Punjabi Market area of Main Street were the only exceptions. The suburbs were distinct and concentrated: there were large Punjabi communities in Surrey and Abbotsford; the Chinese resided largely in Richmond. On my first day of work, I rode the SeaBus, a small ferry, across Vancouver's harbour. I was thinking about the *Komagata Maru* when the ferry passed a Japanese container ship—another *Maru*—anchored at almost the same spot the first one would have been in 1914. Perhaps my quest to understand the history of the *Komagata Maru* started to take shape as I commemorated its long-forgotten presence by pointing my camera and triggering the past.

On May 23, 1914, the *Komagata Maru* arrived in Vancouver's harbour. The Japanese-owned ship had been chartered by a Sikh entrepreneur, Gurdit Singh, to carry South Asian immigrants to Canada. On board were 376 passengers, comprising 340 Sikhs, 24 Muslims and 12 Hindus. These migrants from British India believed that, as British subjects, it was their right to settle anywhere in the British Empire. Britain had repeatedly assured them of their equality.

Instead, the ship was forced to anchor half a mile off Vancouver's shore, and the passengers were detained. Thus began a dramatic standoff that would escalate over the next two months. The story of the *Komagata Maru* became one of the most infamous "incidents" in Canadian history. But it was far from incidental. The event was the culmination of a long history of attempts to prevent South Asians from entering Canada.

Canadian authorities did not give the migrants a reason for their detention. They were denied full access to legal counsel. They were driven to the brink of desperate thirst and starvation. These tactics were designed to force Gurdit Singh and the ship's passengers to turn back of their own accord, so that they could not raise a legal challenge in Canadian courts. British imperial interests defined Canada's response. Distinct identities with well-defined borders were encouraged and officially sanctioned in British India, and the British responded with great deliberateness to each of these identities in a different way. Laws and regulations were enacted in various parts of the world, including Canada, to prevent the immigration of the peoples of British India. The region, known today as South Asia, includes not only India but Pakistan, Bangladesh, Sri Lanka and Nepal. Organizations such as the BBC also include Afghanistan. Canada's South Asian community at the time was largely Punjabi and Sikh, and Sikh and Punjabi Muslim soldiers made up most of the British Indian Army, a key component of British occupation. Most of the passengers of the *Komagata Maru* had army connections, as did many members of Canada's South Asian community. Canada was advised to be cautious, so that British India, and especially the "native" army, would not be inflamed by overt racism.

In 1908, Canada had added the "continuous journey" regulation to its Immigration Act. The new regulation required that all immigrants had to come to Canada by direct journey from their country of birth or citizenship. The neutral language was employed deliberately to hide the regulation's true intent: the barring of immigrants from British India. Between 1908 and 1914, it proved astonishingly effective. The year before the regulation came into force, just over 2,600 South Asians had entered Canada. Afterwards, only a few dozen had managed to enter.

On the basis of this regulation, the court ruled that the passengers on the *Komagata Maru* could not land. As a self-governing dominion in the British Empire, the court asserted, Canada had the right to determine who got in. It could also

RIGHT Upon Ali Kazimi's first visit to Vancouver in 1986, he photographed this Japanese ship, another *Maru*, in the harbour close to where the *Komagata Maru* was anchored more than seven decades earlier. All Japanese ships use the suffix *maru*, which means circle in Japanese.

legally bar immigrants on the basis of race. The *Komagata Maru* was the first ship carrying migrants to be turned away from Canadian shores, and the event would set a precedent for the century to come.

In 1939, a German steamship, the *St. Louis*, arrived on the east coast of North America carrying 937 Europeans, mostly German Jews fleeing the Nazi pogroms. After Cuba denied them landing, Canada, along with the United States, did not extend its welcome. Supported by Prime Minister William Lyon Mackenzie King, Frederick Charles Blair, head of the Immigration Branch of the Department of Mines and Resources, took the position that "no country could open its doors wide enough to take in the hundreds of thousands of Jewish people who want to leave Europe: the line must be drawn somewhere." Two hundred and fifty-four of the passengers aboard the *St. Louis* would perish in Nazi concentration camps.

By contrast, in 1948, 347 European refugees, mainly Estonians, arrived in Halifax aboard the *Walnut*, fleeing Soviet oppression. They were met with open arms. Today there is a special display at Pier 21, the location of the national immigration museum in Halifax, dedicated to their voyage and arrival.[6]

In fact, the differentiation between "desirable" and "undesirable" immigrants was embedded in Canada's official immigration policies from the time of Confederation. In the hand-wringing over current immigration policies, it is rare for anyone to acknowledge that the Canadian nation state was self-consciously shaped through racist immigration policies. These are referred to as "exclusions," a term that both acknowledges and hides the goal of establishing a "white man's country," which was pursued by Canada in its first hundred years. These exclusions were both external and internal, of course. Canada was created through the colonization of aboriginal people, and their participation in the Canadian nation state was never imagined or actively sought. People often flinch when I speak of Canada as a "white settler state." It is naming the whiteness of the enterprise that causes discomfort, and the history explored in this book is rooted in that uncomfortable space.

The "White Canada" policy was finally dismantled in 1967, when all references to race were removed from Canada's Immigration Act and a points system was implemented. At the same time, immigration officers were given wide discretionary powers for selection. Canadian embassies continued to be concentrated in the "traditional source" countries. In 1972, 4,420 carefully selected South Asians fleeing repression in Uganda were allowed to come to Canada. There was an immense public backlash, and the "Ugandan Asian issue" proved costly for Prime Minister Pierre Trudeau and the Liberals. In the ensuing election, they lost their majority in

the House of Commons. The first act of the resulting minority government was to
suspend the ability of anyone visiting Canada to apply for immigrant status.[7] An
immediate result was the turning away of dozens of South Asians arriving at the
Toronto airport.[8] A *Globe and Mail* editorial approved of these restrictions, claiming
that, among other things, "such a loose system must have admitted many undesirables."[9] This political lesson has not been forgotten. Race and immigration are
intrinsically intertwined in the Canadian public sphere, and governments continue
to respond to perceived public backlash by passing restrictive immigration policies.

While "processing targets" for immigrants to Canada have slowly been shifting
to Asia over the past two decades, temporary work permits have been issued more
and more often. In the past few years, temporary foreign workers have begun to
outnumber new permanent residents to Canada.[10] These workers are sought only for
their labour, much like Asian men were in the nineteenth and twentieth centuries.
Since the mid-eighties, the occasional arrival of ships carrying refugees has been
met with strong public opposition. The ensuing moral panic has allowed federal
governments of all political stripes to pass legislation that makes Canada's immigration and refugee policies increasingly restrictive. The media frequently labels
these migrants queue-jumpers and disregards their asylum claims, even though,
as a signatory to international humanitarian laws, Canada has obligations to the
refugees who arrive on its shores. Although most Canadians descend from people
who arrived by ship, these new migrants are often referred to as "boat people." All of
the recent ships have carried non-European migrants; their passengers have been
of South Asian (Sikh and Tamil) and Chinese (Fujian) origin. The history of the
Komagata Maru resonates with each new arrival.

For decades, members of Canada's Sikh community pressed for a public apology from the federal government for the *Komagata Maru* "incident." Prime Minister Stephen Harper did apologize in 2008 at an annual community event in Surrey, B.C.: the Gadri Babian Da Mela, which commemorates Ghadar Party revolutionaries. No government official seemed to have noticed the irony of the prime minister, a staunch proponent of the "war on terror," offering his apology at an event celebrating those the British Empire considered to be seditionists and terrorists.

Many in the Sikh community were angry that Harper's apology was not offered in the House of Commons. The Canadian government has made apologies from the floor of the House regarding the head tax imposed on Chinese immigrants, the internment of Japanese Canadians and the residential school system to which aboriginal people were subjected. However, it is worthwhile to question whether such forms of national contrition adequately resolve the issues that underlie these so-called "dark chapters" in Canada's history, especially since many past practices either continue or have manifested themselves in new forms. The Safe Third Country Agreement, for example, signed in 2002 between Canada and United States, echoes the continuous journey regulation in its requirement that people seeking asylum must arrive directly from their country of citizenship. In the first two years after the agreement's implementation in 2004, refugee claims at the Canada-U.S. border dropped by more than 43 per cent.[11]

A close examination of Canada's response to the arrival of the *Komagata Maru* reveals motifs that are all too familiar today. The ship's passengers were denied due process and full access to legal counsel; they were anchored in Vancouver's harbour but considered to be poised on the Canadian border; they were confined to the ship but not considered detained—in essence, left dangling in a place of physical and legal ambiguity. The *Komagata Maru*'s passengers were alleged to be seditious, posing a threat to the British Empire. The press was barred from the ship, increasing the passengers' isolation. Concerned that the courts could not be trusted to deliver the results it sought, the federal government tried to circumvent the law, employing a deliberate strategy of delay to wear down the passengers' resolve.[12]

Compare the arrival on Canadian shores of yet another ship in August 2010, the *Sun Sea*, carrying 492 Sri Lankan Tamils seeking asylum. The ship's passengers were held in detention and denied access to legal counsel; the media were kept away. Concerns about terrorist links and national security were added to the existing stereotypes of "queue-jumpers," "bogus claimants" and "economic migrants."

The moral panic generated among members of the public was exploited to create support for Bill c-49, legislation ostensibly proposed to stop human smuggling, which is currently being debated in the House of Commons. Legal experts and refugee groups have denounced the bill, charging that it "flagrantly violates the Canadian Charter of Rights and Canada's international legal obligations."[13] If passed, the law would allow some refugee claimants, including children, to be jailed for up to a year without a review of their cases. Even those accepted as refugees would be barred from gaining permanent residence for five years, during which period they would not be able to leave Canada or bring their spouses or children into the country.

The precedents set by the events surrounding the *Komagata Maru* continue to haunt Canada's immigration and refugee framework. Is it possible that a century from now Canada will be offering apologies for the events of today?

LEFT This map, from the *Imperial Gazetteer,* of what is known today as South Asia shows the British Indian Empire in 1909 divided into territories administered by colonial authorities and hundreds of smaller princely states, which were semi-autonomous but controlled by the British.

1 ─────

MIGRATIONS AND
THE MYTH OF EMPIRE

ON JUNE 22, 1897, hundreds of troops from across the British Empire gathered in London to celebrate the Diamond Jubilee of Queen Victoria. The military procession was a spectacle. It displayed the empire's might and unity and the acquiescence of diverse national populations to British rule. The parade also bolstered the myth of equality among the empire's assorted subjects.

The South Asian contingents that marched in the streets of London were attired in regimental uniforms that blended East and West: specifically shaped and tied turbans, westernized kurtas and cummerbunds combined with western trousers and belts. To the uninitiated eye, those marching may have looked quite similar. In reality, they were men of different backgrounds. Most were Sikhs and Muslims from the region of Punjab or Muslim Pashtuns from the northwest. Regularly glorified by the British as "martial races," these men formed a majority in the British Indian Army. The two groups were also represented in other colonial contingents in the parade. Their reputation allowed thousands of the men to easily gain security-related employment not only in British India but also in British-controlled areas of Asia. Some became policemen in Hong Kong, China or Singapore. Others took posts as security guards for private businesses or joined the military forces in the Federated Malay States.

After the pomp and pageantry of the jubilee celebrations, the South Asian contingents returned to British India. The troops from Hong Kong and the Malay

ABOVE Diamond Jubilee celebrations, 1897, London. A contingent of British Indian Army cavalry officers is seen ahead of Queen Victoria's carriage. Toronto's *Globe* newspaper reported that while it was one thing to see British troops from all over the world, it was quite another to see "shoulder by shoulder, Australian and Houssa [*sic*], Canadian and Sikh."

RIGHT Sikh soldiers of the Malay States Guides.

FAR RIGHT Punjabi Muslim soldiers of the Hong Kong Regiment. The soldiers in both photographs were among the first South Asians to pass through Canada, on their way back from London to Southeast Asia.

Supplement to THE ARMY & NAVY GAZETTE, Saturday, December 1st, 1900.

MILITARY TYPES—No. 156.

TYPES OF FORCES IN THE SMALLER COLONIES.

NORTH BORNEO DYAK POLICE.   MALAY STATES GUIDES.   MAURITIUS GARRISON ARTILLERY.   HONG-KONG SIKH POLICE.   HONG-KONG CHINESE-POLICE.
Sergeant.

States boarded a westbound ship that would take them home via Atlantic Canada. In Montreal, the troops boarded trains for Vancouver, from which Canadian Pacific (CP) ships would carry them back to Singapore or Hong Kong.[1] A report in the *Toronto Star* on August 16, 1897, indicated that some of the contingent was planning to stop in Toronto to march in the Canadian Diamond Jubilee parade at the Industrial Exhibition (later renamed the Canadian National Exhibition). "The Sikhs of the Malay States will also be represented. These troops are Mohammedans and come principally from Ceylon and the Malay settlements," said the article. The reporter conflated Sikhs and "Mohammedans," the common Victorian English name for Muslims; the Federated Malay States employed both. The *Toronto Star* report is the first known written mention of a group of South Asians setting foot in Canada.[2]

These celebrations of empire hid the underlying and growing tensions between the mother country and her white colonies. That same year, Britain had pressured Canada to give it preferential trade benefits, and customs duties on British goods were lowered 25 per cent below the general rate. Poet Rudyard Kipling deftly distilled meaning from this seemingly innocuous event:

ABOVE South Asians, particularly Sikhs and Punjabi Muslims, served in the security forces of British territories across Asia. Many South Asian immigrants who were veterans continued to wear parts of their regimental uniforms after arriving in Canada, as a mark of their loyalty and service to the empire.

A Nation spoke to a Nation,
A Queen sent word to a Throne:
"Daughter am I in my mother's house,
But mistress in my own.
The gates are mine to open,
As the gates are mine to close,
And I set my house in order,"
Said our Lady of the Snows.[3]

Canada was indeed breaking slowly away from Britain, and it would assert control over its own gates before long.

The abolition of slavery in 1838 had created an acute shortage of cheap labour in various parts of the British Empire, particularly in the plantation economies of sugar, tea and rubber in the New World. This gave rise to the practice of indentured labour, in which migrant workers were recruited for contractually fixed periods of time. Historian Hugh Tinker has described indenture as "a new system of slavery."[4] But for able-bodied men and women in desperate financial situations or facing starvation, indentured labour may have seemed a better deal. The terms set out for indentured labourers were simple. The plantation owners paid for the workers' passage; in return, the migrants served for five years. At the end of their contract, the workers were free to either return to their homeland or settle in the colony they had been taken to. Most did not or could not return home.

Beginning in the 1800s, British India provided much of the indentured labour for the colonies. Labourers recruited from poor regions in eastern and southern British India were sent by the tens of thousands to places like British Guiana, Trinidad, Jamaica, Mauritius, Natal (South Africa) and Fiji. A large number of the workers who went to the Caribbean, Mauritius and the Seychelles were drawn from what are now the Indian states of Uttar Pradesh and Bihar. By 1919, an estimated 1.5 million South Asians had migrated across the British Empire.[5]

The experience of migrating to unknown parts of the world was varied. Many traditional, high-caste Hindus referred to the seas as *kala paani* (dark water). Since voyaging across the ocean would result in the permanent loss of one's "caste," or hereditary social position, only those among the higher castes who were desperate chose this option. For the lower castes, however, who were already at the margins of Hindu society, caste restrictions may have been an incentive to move. There were no such cultural or religious barriers among Muslims and Sikhs.

South Asian women were allowed into colonies such as Jamaica, as indentured labourers, but were barred from Britain's "white colonies" to discourage permanent settlement. South Asian and Chinese migrants in many parts of the British Empire were referred to as "coolies," a term for unskilled labourers that became a racial slur.

BELOW An indentured South Asian worker on a rubber plantation in Fiji in the early 1900s. Between 1879 and 1916, thousands of men and women were taken to Fiji as *girmityas* (indentured workers) to work on sugar cane and rubber plantations. The system of indenture was abolished on January 1, 1920.

4831 Jamaica, Coolie man and woman,

ABOVE An extended South Asian family, with an African man holding horses. The man on the far right is wearing a *dhoti,* a traditional garment. The photo was taken in the late 1890s in the town of Umzinto, near the coast of what was then the colony of Natal and is now KwaZulu-Natal province, South Africa.

LEFT An albumen print from the 1890s, showing a harbour in British India. Steamships were essential for transporting raw materials to Britain and returning to India with finished goods. Some ships also carried migrants, both indentured and free, to faraway colonies in the Caribbean and to Fiji.

RIGHT Soldiers—sepoys—of the British East India Company's army in the early 1800s. Typically for the period, the soldiers are dressed in European-style uniforms. After the uprising of 1857–58, the image of the sepoy would be replaced by that of the stalwart Sikh.

BELOW Members of Hodson's Horse, a body of loyal Indian horsemen formed during the Indian Mutiny (1857–58). This Felice Beato photograph was likely taken in March 1858, after the capture of the city of Lucknow.

BY THE MID-NINETEENTH century, the British East India Company had consolidated its hold over most of South Asia. The Sikh Kingdom of Punjab, the last major territory to hold out, was annexed in 1849 after the Second Anglo-Sikh War. The relentless British expansion in South Asia was made possible through the British Indian Army, which was made up of locally recruited "sepoys"—the word derives from *sipahi*, Persian for soldier—who were trained, clothed and equipped in the European style and led by British officers.

At the same time, exploitative taxes, controls imposed on local industry to open the market to English products and the growing power of evangelical Christian groups were fuelling discontent among the South Asian populace. In 1857, things came to a head—and the first eruption was among the sepoys in the army. The sepoys were unhappy with their pay, and there were anxieties over the loss of caste in the case of overseas deployment. But the spark that ignited the uprising was the new ammunition the army had introduced, which required a soldier to tear off the top of the cartridge with his teeth in order to load his rifle. Rumours spread that the grease in the cartridge was animal fat, derived from both cows and pigs. Most Hindus do not eat beef, and Muslims are forbidden from eating pork. The soldiers felt betrayed, and a number of regiments mutinied.

ABOVE A rare hand-tinted portrait of a Sikh soldier of Hodson's Horse, taken by photographer Felice Beato in Lucknow, 1858. Many Sikhs, particularly those from the Cis-Sutlej region of Punjab, and Punjabi Muslims joined the British in quelling the uprising.

Although many units of the British Indian Army remained loyal, more troops were needed to put down the spreading rebellion. Tapping into and exacerbating historic grievances to build alliances was a carefully refined British strategy. A British Indian rebellion would have to be countered using people who felt themselves to be on the outside, and in the mid-1800s the peoples of the Punjab and the North-west Frontier Province still saw themselves as distinct and different from those of the Indo-Gangetic Plains. Veterans of the Sikh armies, particularly in the Cis-Sutlej region, were battle-hardened and available. New regiments were raised, many of which included Punjabi Muslims and Pashtuns in their ranks.

Nothing caught the imagination of the British public more than horrific stories of the rape and massacre of European women during the uprising. The depravity of the "natives," as graphically narrated in the newspapers, confirmed people's worst fears

about the heathen hordes Britain was trying to civilize. Never mind that most of these sensational stories were fabricated.[6] The public mood they generated allowed for a genocidal British response, and horrific bloodletting was unleashed.

British author Christopher Herbert, in his critically acclaimed book *War of No Pity,* contends that the British were traumatized by their own response:

> The Mutiny… inflicted its wound on the British psyche not merely by confronting it with spectacles of terrifying physical violence but also fundamentally by inflicting upon it the shock of what seemed to be a catastrophic wound to the moral order itself. If I am reading the Mutiny Literature correctly, the discovery of the strain of genocidal cruelty inhabiting humanitarian Christian virtue and linking the British inseparably to "those red-handed Sepoys" formed an essential component of this horror.[7]

The rule of the British East India Company was abolished in 1858, once the rebellion was put down. Britain took direct control of its Indian territory. While recognizing that they could not hold onto their empire without the British Indian Army, the British knew the army had to be reinvented. Loyalty to the Crown had to be instilled, just as moral justification for colonization and imperial rule had to be found. In British India a new theory of "martial races" emerged. Peoples were now

ABOVE This 1858 watercolour by Orlando Norie shows two sepoys about to be "blown from cannons" by the Bengal Horse Artillery. These public executions were designed to strike terror in the minds of colonial subjects. Sikh cavalry appear behind the British troops on the left; Sikh loyalty was highlighted at every opportunity.

RIGHT Soldiers of the Twenty-third Sikh Pioneers charge Abyssinian (Ethiopian) troops in the Battle of Arogee Ravine, 1868. The British Indian Army, referred to as "the sword arm of the British Empire," was used to expand and protect British imperial interests.

to be classified according to their "warlike traits." The people of the Punjab—primarily Sikhs and members of the majority population, Punjabi Muslims—were deemed to be "martial classes," as were the Pashtuns and Afridi tribesmen to the northwest and the Gurkhas from the Himalayan kingdom of Nepal, among a few other select groups.

The delicately balanced imperial order rested on a foundation of divide-and-rule. In 1858 the Punjab Committee on Reorganization's report summed it up with precision: "Next to the grand counterpoise of a sufficient European force, comes the counterpoise of natives against natives."[8]

The revamped and reorganized British Indian Army became a mainly Punjabi force, supplemented with men from the other "martial races." The public face of the Indian Army now was the stalwart bearded-and-turbaned Sikh soldier. The British Indian Army, "the sword arm of the British Empire," was used not only to police the British Empire in India and fight ongoing battles on its frontiers, but also to expand British rule in parts of the Middle East, China, Southeast Asia and Africa. As a safeguard, the British ensured that the more than seventy thousand white troops serving with the British Army in India always had weaponry one generation ahead of the weapons used by the British Indian Army.

According to Philip Mason, in the seminal work *A Matter of Honour,* the British Indian Army was far more than simply a mercenary force. It became an efficient and unquestioning professional force through drill and discipline, under the organization and leadership of British officers. The peasants and farmers who joined the army were bound first by loyalty to comrades with whom they shared linguistic and caste ties. They fought to preserve personal *izzat,* honour and integrity to their oath of loyalty to the British Crown. Every regiment became an extension of family. The British officers, expected to learn the language of the men they commanded and to be aware of their cultural norms, wore ceremonial uniforms that included turbans and kurtas. The soldiers were never seen outside a paternalistic framework of Anglo-Saxon superiority; they were courageous, but nonetheless simple-minded and

1st Duke of York's Own Lancers (Skinner's Horse)

45th Rattrays Sikhs (Drum Major)

Artillery Gunner Mountain Battery.

Queens Own Corps of Guides (Cavalry) Duffadar

LEFT British Indian Army troops, with their spectacularly colourful uniforms and turbans, were much sought after as subjects for British artists and postcard publishers. By the end of the nineteenth century, the majority of troops were recruited from the Punjab.

BELOW This illustration of the Nineteenth Punjabis, a Punjabi Muslim regiment of the British Indian Army, shows the evolution of their uniforms from their traditional dress (seen in the middle). The term "khaki," Hindustani for dust-coloured, comes from the colour of the British Indian Army field uniforms.

19th Punjabis.

RIGHT Men and children from an extended Sikh family whose members served in the Bengal Lancers pose during the 1890s. British Indian Army regiments liked to recruit men from the same family to ensure loyalty across generations. Employment in the army offered many privileges, along with a sense of honour.

BELOW British Indian Army troops were part of the allied forces that put down the Boxer Rebellion in China in 1901–2, and many of them remained stationed there. In this 1906 photograph, the Forty-seventh Sikhs, led by bagpipers and drummers, march through Tianjin (Tientsin at that time), in northern China.

childlike. They were encouraged to be dependent on the British Crown, which was described to them as *sircar mai-baap* (the government that is mother and father).

In 1877 Queen Victoria was declared the Empress of India, and presented as the protector, benefactor and sovereign of the people of British India rather than as a foreign queen. The governor general of India was now to be called the viceroy. As the direct representative of the Crown, he was invested with far more powers over the people of British India than the queen held over hers in Britain.

BY THE LATE nineteenth century, South Asians were migrating to parts of the empire not necessarily linked to the indentured labour system. Traders and labourers from the western coast region of Gujarat and the southern Tamil-speaking

BELOW It was common to see South Asian policemen in British territories all over Southeast Asia. Sikhs, Punjabi Muslims and men belonging to the other few groups the British classed as "martial races" found it easy to get security-related work.

RIGHT South Asian policemen became a familiar feature in the International Treaty Settlement of Shanghai and British treaty ports in China. Once their contracts were up, some of the ex-policemen headed for Canada and the United States.

BELOW Sikh and Muslim British Indian Army veterans, survivors of the 1857–58 campaigns, brought together for a reunion in 1903 to celebrate the coronation of Edward VII the previous year as emperor of British India. The threat of another mutiny haunted British policy until India achieved independence in 1947.

Indian Police Force in Foreign Settlement in China.

region had begun to settle in eastern and southern Africa. South Asian migration to southern Africa was of a magnitude that prompted British white settlers to pressure the colonial government to stem the tide. The issue was a delicate one. In 1895, Joseph Chamberlain, British secretary of state for the colonies, acknowledged that any attempt to create a policy of exclusion on the basis of race would have a significant political impact in India. So the British devised indirect methods in order to mask their intention. Among them was the Natal Dictation Test, named after the colony of Natal in South Africa where it was first devised.[9] Immigration officials could administer dictation tests to all new arrivals in any known European language. Mohandas Karamchand Gandhi, then a young lawyer, mobilized the Indian community

in South Africa to fight against the discriminatory process. A protracted struggle ended in a gentlemen's agreement that limited the number of Indians allowed into South Africa.

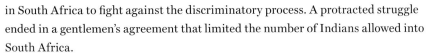

ABOVE   A medal commemorating the White Australia policy. The map of Australia is made of the newly introduced and highly prized white metal aluminum. Imperial authorities discouraged Canada from naming its immigration policy in a similar fashion, though the results were nearly identical.

As the United States developed its own race-based restrictions, Canada looked to other colonies within the empire for ideas and strategies. A few dozen South Asians had been brought to Australia in 1834. In 1860, Pashtuns, Baluchis and Afridis, from the regions bordering Afghanistan, and some Punjabi Muslims were brought in with their trained camels, which were essential for the exploration of the outback. Australians called them all "Afghans."[10] By the end of the century, two thousand South Asian men were working as "cameleers." There were also small, widely dispersed pockets of Hindus and Sikhs. However, the more numerous Chinese were the government's first targets. Since 1855 the Australian colony of Victoria had successfully curtailed Chinese immigration with the imposition of a poll tax on every Chinese arrival. In 1885 Canada used this as a model for the Chinese Head Tax.

The new Commonwealth of Australia, formed in 1901, immediately devised a clearly articulated White Australia policy, effectively employing the Natal Dictation Test as a tool. New Zealand later followed suit, with many in Canada also clamouring for the Australian model. The province of British Columbia tried on

CERTIFICATE EXEMPTING FROM DICTATION TEST.

Book No. 96

Form No. 21. **COMMONWEALTH OF AUSTRALIA.** No. 100
DUPLICATE. *Immigration Restriction Acts 1901-1905 and Regulations.* 78/1913

I, *Oswald Septimus Maddock* the Collector of Customs for the State of *Western Australia* in the said Commonwealth, hereby certify that *Shah Kail* hereinafter described, who is leaving the Commonwealth temporarily, will be excepted from the provisions of paragraph (g) of Section 3 of the Act if he returns to the Commonwealth within a period of *36 months* from this date.

O. S. Maddock

Date *28· 3 ·1913*
                                          Collector of Customs.

DESCRIPTION

Nationality *Afghan*   Birthplace *Peshwar*
Age *41 Years*   Complexion *Dark*
Height *5 Feet 5¾"*   Hair *Black*
Build *Medium*   Eyes *Dark brown*
Particular marks *Scar on left cheek*

(For impression of hand see back of this document.)

PHOTOGRAPHS.

Full Face :—   Profile :—

Date of departure *29 · 3 · 13*   Destination *Colombo*
Ship *Friedrich der Grosse*
Date of return   Ship
Port
                                          Customs Officer

FAR LEFT From 1860 on, camels were exported from British India to Australia. With them went cameleers, mostly Muslim men from the Pashtun, Afridi, Hazara and Punjabi ethnic groups living along India's border regions with Afghanistan, as well as some Sikhs. Cameleers were instrumental in opening up the Australian outback for settlement. Many of these "Afghans" were veterans of the British Indian Army.

LEFT This travel document was issued to all Asians who were living in Australia before the White Australia policy came into effect in 1901. After that, all Asian immigrants had to write a dictation test, showing proficiency in a European language. The certificate shown is for a Pashtun man, Shah Kail, who was born in the city of Peshawar, in what is today Pakistan.

ABOVE A Sikh man shears an Australian sheep using an electric tool in the early 1910s. South Asian servants were brought to the Australian colonies as early as 1837. According to the 1911 census, there were 3,698 South Asians in Australia, including a small but widely dispersed Sikh community.

ABOVE A painting of Vancouver's harbour in the early 1900s, with the Canadian Pacific Railway pier and station in the foreground, by contemporary Canadian artist John Horton. The immigration shed is located immediately past the bow of the docked CP ship, the *Empress of Japan*.

RIGHT Native longshoremen pose in front of four lumber-carrying ships in Vancouver, 1889. South Asian troops passing through Vancouver's harbour at the turn of the nineteenth century would have seen perhaps the most culturally diverse workplace in Canada.

several occasions to adopt the Natal Dictation Test, but each time the legislation was deemed unconstitutional and overruled by the federal government.

In 1902, South Asian troops made another appearance in Canada. A contingent from the Hong Kong Regiment patterned after the British Indian Army, consisting of South Asian Muslim soldiers, arrived at the port of Vancouver. They were en route to England for the coronation of Edward VII, and were travelling on one of CP's Empress line of ships. The Empress ships were floating capsules of diversity, and this voyage was no exception. Also on board were soldiers from the First Chinese Regiment of the British Army, along with immigrants from Japan. The crew, as was typically the case on CP's ships, consisted of Chinese seamen and white officers. In Vancouver's harbour, the South Asian soldiers would have witnessed a different mix of people: aboriginal and Chinese longshoremen working side by side; aboriginal, Japanese and European fishermen hauling in their catches. The very next year, the colonial landscape of British Columbia would include South Asians from British India.

Vancouver in the early 1900s was a frontier city of about fifty thousand people. Just over half its population was male and Anglo-Saxon, but it was still the most culturally diverse city in Canada, albeit with deep racial divides. Racial violence had reshaped the geography of the city. Euphemisms like "Chinatown" and "Japantown" masked the reality of segregated areas defined by apartheid-like lines that were enforced by the occasional riot." Chinatown was largely male. The Japanese part of town had more women and children. At the margins of the city lay several aboriginal communities.

Punjabi immigrants started arriving in British Columbia around 1903. Most of the new arrivals were veterans of the British Indian Army, or had served in the Malay States, Hong Kong or Singapore. The non-commissioned South Asian officers among them would have known at least a smattering of English. In turn, white officers who had retired to Canada would have spoken poor but understandable Hindustani, the language spoken across much of northern British India.

ABOVE Lord Kitchener and the Duke of Connaught (in the white pith helmet) inspecting an officer of the British Indian Army at King Edward VII's coronation in 1902. The Duke of Connaught would go on to serve as Canada's governor general from 1911 to 1916 and was in office when the *Komagata Maru* arrived.

ABOVE This snapshot, taken with a Kodak box camera by an unknown American tourist, shows a group of Sikh men conferring after landing at the Vancouver CPR station in the early 1900s. Word had spread through the army contingents that as British subjects they could settle in this part of the empire.

Newspaper accounts and letters indicate that a few former British officers conversed with the new arrivals, and in some cases helped them get work or petitioned the authorities on their behalf.

There is no certainty about who was the first South Asian to arrive in Canada. In 1907, a Sikh immigrant to Vancouver made the following claim to the *Daily Province:*

> It was a Mohammedan who drifted here four years ago from Hong Kong and did well who started the tide. Those who followed him did equally well, and today… Hindus are labouring in factories, earning a good wage by doing work which whites refuse to do, law abiding and contented.[12]

The South Asian immigrants referred to themselves as Hindustanis, which meant the people of Hindustan, a colloquial name for the region of British India. Canadians and Americans shortened this to "Hindus," also spelled "Hindoos." The term handily allowed people to avoid confusion in distinguishing South Asian arrivals from North America's native "Indians."

LEFT A Sikh man, upon landing in Vancouver. Like European immigrants, South Asians were coming to Canada for a better life—but that fact mattered little to officials. The issue was "desirability," and South Asians were undesirable.

ABOVE This photograph from the 1890s is of the Canadian Pacific Railway train station and wharf in Vancouver's harbour. The end of the transcontinental railway line marked the start of the trans-Pacific shipping line. An Empress-class ship is docked at the pier in the background.

In 1904, the arrival of close to sixty "Hindoos" in Vancouver caused much alarm. Municipal authorities were disturbed enough to send the following complaint to the secretary of state in Ottawa, R.W. Scott:

Sir,

It has been brought to the attention of the civic authorities that a large number of East Indians are being brought to this city from the Orient by transportation companies, and many of them afterwards become a charge of the city and Province. It is stated that they are brought here under false pretences and are led to believe that they can secure immediate employment at wages far beyond the dreams of an Oriental in his own country. It is felt by the city that some steps should be taken by the proper authorities to disillusion these people, and if possible, to punish those who are the means of bringing them here.

I have been instructed to write you with that object in view, and trust you may devise some plan to shut out this element, who are naturally unfitted to stand this climate which is so different from their own, and which rapidly incapacitates them for manual labour, even if there were abundance of it.

I have the honour to be, Sir,

Your obedient servant,

Thos. F. McGuigan

City Clerk[13]

McGuigan's letter contains two claims that would become ubiquitous in popular media and would later be embedded in Canadian immigration policy: South Asian immigrants had been lured to Canada by shipping company agents, and they were physically unsuited to the country's climate.

By 1906, there were just over 2,500 South Asians in British Columbia, which had a total population of about 100,000. The overwhelming majority of those South Asians were Sikhs, who'd had considerable incentive to leave home. In the Punjab, as in other parts of India, drought, famine and disease pandemics were wreaking havoc, and the colonial government was doing little to alleviate the situation. Exports of food supplies to Britain continued unabated even during these periods of acute deprivation. Exorbitant taxes forced farmers to seek loans from moneylenders who charged usurious interest rates. Millions lost their land to creditors. Apart from joining the army or the police force, the only way to hold onto one's land was to send someone from the family abroad to work for higher wages.

As one South Asian immigrant told Fred Lockley of the *Pacific Monthly* in 1907,

Hunger, actual hunger, is what is bringing my fellow-countrymen here. In India the wages are low, unbelievably low, so low that it is hard work to keep body and soul together. During times of famine the British government gives relief work, paying four cents a day to the men and three cents a day to the women. For work on the streets and similar work the usual wage is about $2.25 a month. Naturally these men who have seen other parts of the world realize that they can do better away from home and hence come here. They prefer to come to a country under the British flag, for many of them have fought for that flag in the hill wars in India, in Egypt, in the Boxer troubles in China, and in the Boer war in South Africa. They see the English people received gladly and welcomed royally in India, and they suppose that, having borne the brunt of England's wars in the Far East, they will be welcomed wherever the British flag is flying. But it seems they are mistaken. I have travelled all over Asia and I have not heard a word or read a notice in all my travels inviting my countrymen to come to Canada. They have heard of this as a country where a man has all he needs to eat, so they come.[14]

The fact that, like European immigrants, South Asians were coming to Canada for a better life mattered little. The issue was "desirability," and South Asians were undesirable. The "Hindu Invasion," as it was known in the press, further fuelled the hysteria that resulted from growing Chinese and Japanese immigration (dubbed the "yellow peril"). It took less than five years for public opinion, backed by local and provincial governments, to convince the federal government that a way of blocking South Asian entry into Canada had to be devised. The course of action was not obvious, however, since South Asians were fellow British subjects—in 1907, Canadians were still British subjects and carried British passports. Back in 1891 Sir John A. Macdonald, the country's first prime minister, had famously declared, "A British subject I was born—a British subject I will die," and that attitude prevailed into the new century.[15] Yet at this juncture Britain could ill afford Canada asserting its whiteness.

LEFT Many lumber mills in B.C. employed South Asians, like the Sikh workers in this photograph. Lumber mill owners were looking for cheap, reliable labourers in order to maintain their profit margins. White labour groups were opposed to South Asians working for lower wages, and to the fact that the recent immigrants seemed to save money by living communally.

2

BUILDING CANADA AS A "WHITE MAN'S COUNTRY"

THE EARLY DECADES of the twentieth century witnessed dramatic population growth for Canada. A country of just over five million people, it accepted, on average, more than 200,000 immigrants from Europe and the U.S. every year between 1908 and 1914.

In the competition for new immigrants, Canada vied with other former colonies and settler states, including the United States. It offered the greatest incentives to Britons, northern Europeans and western Europeans, in that order. Massive advertising campaigns were mounted, enticing potential immigrants with the prospect of free passage to Canada and ample land to settle on. When the favoured sources started to dry up, Canada opened its doors to eastern and southern Europeans, among them persecuted groups such as Mennonites, Doukhobors and Hutterites.

Canada's immigration strategy was based on the desire to build a nation imagined as a "white man's country." As law professor Audrey Macklin has pointed out, during this era "the doctrine of white racial superiority was an ideological force pervading every level of Canadian society almost without exception."[1]

The Chinese immigrants, mostly men, who had been arriving in British Columbia since the 1850s continued to face tremendous hostility. In 1883, Prime Minister John A. Macdonald empathized publicly with Australia in regard to the "permanent entry of a foreign race." He was pragmatic about the Chinese in Canada, however, advocating what he described as "a middle path" while also exhibiting the underlying anxiety about miscegenation that coursed through Victorian Canada.

ABOVE Galician (Ukrainian) immigrant girls with a Canadian immigration officer. When the flow of "desirable" immigrants from Britain and Northern Europe started drying up, Canada looked to eastern Europe and only reluctantly to southern Europe. The notion of "whiteness" had its own hierarchy.

RIGHT While Canadian Pacific shipping agents were accused by the federal government of inducing South Asians to come to Canada, all shipping companies courted British and northern European immigrants by advertising the incentives offered by the government.

ABOVE The *Stubbenhuk*, later renamed the *Scilia*, was launched on August 13, 1890. Between 1898 and 1913 it ferried thousands of immigrants from Europe to Canada and the United States. The ship was then sold to a Japanese company and renamed the *Komagata Maru*.

It is better to have Chinese labour than no labour at all . . . At any moment when the Legislature of Canada chooses, it can shut down the gate and say, no more immigrants shall come here from China; and then no more immigrants will come, and those in the country at the time will rapidly disappear . . . and therefore there is no fear of a permanent degradation of the country by a mongrel race.[2]

Chinese men had been brought to Canada to complete the most difficult sections of the Canadian Pacific Railway. They were imported as cheap labour, and thousands perished while stitching the country together with a railway line. Canada started by imposing the Chinese head tax soon after the last spike was driven; it was set at $50 in 1885, doubled to $100 in 1900 and then raised to $500 in 1903. (Between 1901 and 1918, Canada collected $18 million from Chinese immigrants in head tax payments; during the same period, it spent $10 million to promote emigration from Europe.[3]) China, while offended by the head tax legislation, exercised little power on the international scene. Canada and its sister colonies could discriminate against the Chinese without significant consequences to the British Empire.

Japanese immigrants had started arriving in British Columbia around 1891. Unlike China, imperial Japan was very important to Britain at the time. In 1894, the two countries signed the Anglo-Japanese Treaty of Commerce and Navigation, which secured free entry for the subjects of both empires. As a self-governing dominion, Canada initially chose not to sign on to the treaty, recognizing its immigration implications. But Britain could not afford to have its colonies or dominions

LEFT This rare early photograph shows Chinese immigrant men aboard a CP Empress-class ship. Many of these men were drawn to North America by gold rushes, first in California and then in British Columbia and Yukon. They dubbed the place Gold Mountain—"Gam Sham" in Cantonese.

BELOW Racist stereotypes and caricatures of Chinese immigrants were prevalent across Canada, as shown in this 1879 cover for the popular *Canadian Illustrated News*.

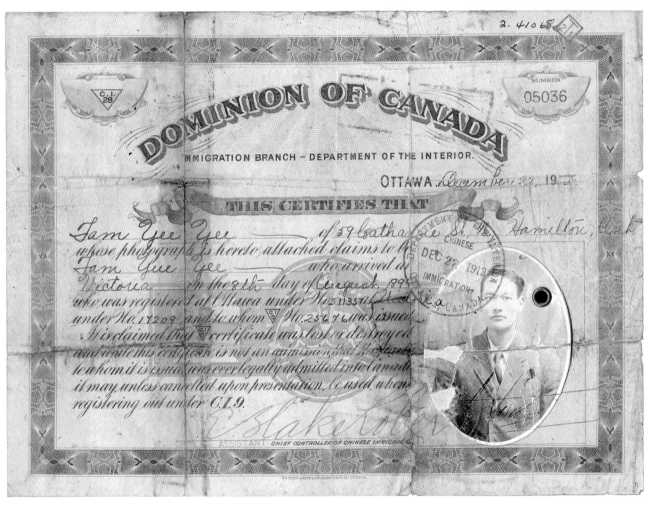

jeopardizing its relationship with a growing world power. As Japanese immigrants to Canada grew in number in the late 1890s, so did the pressure from both Japan and the colonial office in London for Canada to ease their entry. All British Columbia could do was to deny them voting rights, which the government did in 1895. Since they were shut out from most professions by their inability to become full citizens, Japanese immigrants relied heavily on the individual and communal skills of fishing, and successfully built a large fishing fleet. The simmering resentment about their prosperity would explode decades later, with the onset of the Second World War.

Japan's victory in the Russo-Japanese War in 1905 signalled a major shift in global politics. Recognizing the Asian nation's growing power, Britain signed a treaty of cooperation with Japan. The myths of white supremacy began to unravel.

Japan's victory was immensely inspiring for Indian nationalists, whose protests against British rule were getting louder and even more militant. The impact of whites-only immigration policies in the colonies was also starting to have repercussions, particularly in the Punjab, which was still the main recruiting ground for the British Indian Army and other security forces. Britain was alarmed at the growing influence of "agitators," radicals who were calling for a boycott of the entire British system, from taxes to goods and services. Most threatening was the nationalist propaganda that targeted Sikh troops in the British Indian Army, including pamphlets describing the dire conditions of farmers in the Punjab. To counter the threat, British authorities arrested the most powerful and popular Punjabi leaders. Some were "transported for life"—shipped to and imprisoned on the Andaman Islands. Britain also realized there were potentially explosive situations in the colonies, especially Canada. The small but growing South Asian population in British Columbia was overwhelmingly Sikh, and the majority of those men had ties to the British Indian Army. Overt discrimination against them would inflame the delicate situation in Punjab.

The 1906 Immigration Act gave the Canadian government the power to detain or deport anyone deemed to be suffering from disease, and medical examinations became a handy tool for immigration officers seeking to turn away South Asians. Many were detained for treatable conditions such as trachoma and hookworm. Reflecting on how South Asians were treated in Vancouver in those early years, a *New York Times* reporter quoted an unnamed Englishman who had observed immigrants coming before a "kindly" Dominion Immigration Agent:

TOP LEFT Tens of thousands of Chinese workers were brought to Canada to help complete the trans-Canada railway. Thousands perished while working on the dangerous sections running through the Rocky Mountains.

BOTTOM LEFT This head tax certificate for Tam Yee Yee was issued in 1913 to replace a lost original. As with its Australian counterpart, the Certificate for Exemption from the Dictation Test, this certificate's main purpose was to allow Chinese men who had already paid the head tax re-entry into Canada.

RIGHT Many in B.C.'s Japanese community became commercial fishermen and owned boats, like the men in this tourist postcard from the early 1900s. After the outbreak of the war with Japan in 1941, the entire fishing fleet would be confiscated and Japanese Canadians would be sent to internment camps.

BELOW Japanese children buying ice cream from a vendor outside the Imperial Cannery in Vancouver, where many Japanese women worked. Unlike the Chinese and South Asians, Japanese men were allowed to bring in their families. Imperial Japan's alliance with the British Empire tempered Canada's response to Japanese immigration.

AT THE JAPANESE FISHING WHARF, VANCOUVER, B.C.

TOP LEFT Japanese officers pose with an unexploded Russian artillery shell. The bearded General Nogi, a key commander, is seen third from left. Japan's victory in the Russo-Japanese War of 1905 signalled a rise in Asian power and had a significant impact on those struggling for freedom in British India.

BOTTOM LEFT Since Japan was a British ally, Imperial Japanese Navy warships often visited Vancouver, as this one did in 1910. Two warships arrived while the *Komagata Maru* was anchored in Vancouver's harbour but refused to intercede. During the First World War, the Japanese Navy patrolled and protected the west coast of Canada.

The first man examined was a splendid specimen of the Sikh soldier—straight as an arrow, with three medals on his breast, his beard twisted and wound in the Sikh fashion about his ears. He saluted like a piece of machinery, and passed the tests with no trouble. Of those who followed him it was easy to distinguish the old soldiers on account of their correct salutes. The others tried to imitate them but the effect was grotesque. It was, however, surprising to find what a large number were actually old soldiers. None of these were suffering from trachoma, but a few did not have the $25 [the landing fee for immigrants]. It made no difference—out they had to go into the deportation pen. Half a dozen medals gained in the service of the Emperor did not weigh against the lack of even a dollar of the required amount.

The anonymous commentator went on to describe how the people of Vancouver were responding to the South Asian arrivals:

If an Indian went into a barbershop the proprietor was as likely as not to tell him with an oath to get out. They would not, in all probability, be insulted in the streets, but they would be made to feel through small incidents that they were pariahs—unfit to breathe the same air as the white man. The people of British Columbia are by no means naturally cruel, "but we must harden our hearts," they say, "else this province will become an annex of Asia."

The Englishman was prescient in his concluding remarks to the reporter: "Let me warn British Columbians to show respect to those proud old Sikh pensioners. Do not give them the impression that they are exiles in a foreign country. Both races revere the same flag. Do not aid the cause of the disloyal agitator in India."[4] Even at this early juncture, the global ramifications of local racism were being recognized by some.

Discrimination against South Asian migrants was frequently articulated in discussions concerning labour. Lumber mill owners in British Columbia were looking for cheap, reliable labourers to help maintain their profit margins. White labour groups were opposed both to South Asians working for lower wages and to the fact that the recent immigrants seemed to save money by living communally. In the summer of 1906, Superintendent of Immigration William Duncan Scott asked for a report on this issue from the top immigration officer in Vancouver, A.J. Munroe:

August 16, 1906

As competitor for white labour they are the most dangerous we have, as they practically engage in the same class of work as the white labourers do, viz—mill work and street work. They will not engage in domestic labour, gardening and or agricultural work that white men leave untouched, but seek the same lines of employment usually followed by the white labour.

—that the introduction of this class of cheap labour will be the means of excluding the very class of labour that is most essential for the progress and prosperity of the country i.e. white workers, who if paid a fair living wage could settle here, maintain homes and rear families and thoroughly fulfill the duties of citizenship. At the present time a number of our large employers employ cheap coolie labour for the reason that it is cheap and if this supply of cheap labour is increased the possibility of any outside addition to our white population from outside sources becomes greatly lessened.

—that this country can well afford to be guided in this matter by the experiences of the Australian Commonwealth.

A.J. Munroe

Immigration Agent[5]

Many employers did indeed use South Asian immigrants as a way to keep wages low and to undermine the fledgling union movement. But the labour movement was not progressive enough to call for racial equality. Ed Stevenson of the Saskatchewan executive committee of the Trades and Labour Congress of Canada wrote to the secretary of state for the colonies in London in November 19, 1906.

While it is true that the phenomenal development in the West might absorb this class into labour, the workingmen of Canada are unanimous in protesting against such competition. Our standards of living, which have been gained by many plodding years of self denial and painstaking efforts are in jeopardy by the importation of such non-assimible [sic] subjects. Canadian workmen are not now justly compensated for their major vital part in the creation of national prosperity. Hindoos, by their cost and modes of living, constitute a moral and industrial menace in a predominating [sic] Anglo Saxon community, which by much increase in numbers in this case, will result in a worse Imperial aggravation than the South African Coolie Labour troubles.[6]

"Oriental" immigration was a major issue for British Columbia's politicians across party lines. R.G. MacPherson, the incumbent Liberal member of Parliament from

RIGHT Bhag Singh, a key leader of the Vancouver Shore Committee and a member of the Ghadar Party, is shown here with his two-year-old son. In 1914, after the *Komagata Maru* was sent back, Singh was shot and killed in the Sikh temple by a police informant.

FAR RIGHT An artist's rendition of Balwant Singh, British Indian Army veteran and one of the first *granthis* in the Vancouver gurdwara, or Sikh temple. Singh was a member of both the Khalsa Diwan Society and the United India League. Arrested and tried secretly for conspiracy, he was hanged in 1917.

Vancouver, was under considerable pressure from his constituents to have Prime Minister Wilfrid Laurier take a stand. On September 21, 1906, he wrote to Laurier about the influx of immigrants from South Asia:

> You can never make good Canadian citizens out of them or their descendants and it is just as necessary to keep them out as it is to keep out the Chinese. Most of them are big strapping fellows, men who have fought in British regiments in the little Indian wars, but their ideas and their ways are not ours, nor can they ever be so. These people from India come here alone just like the Chinese, and nothing on earth could make them Canadians.[7]

As noted, the community of South Asian migrants that began to form in British Columbia was mainly Punjabi and Sikh in its makeup. Most were army veterans, but there were also farmers, tradesmen and merchants in the mix. Local conditions offered only low-paying, unskilled jobs, but gradually a few South Asians emerged as shopkeepers, real estate agents, even publishers and students. Most lived collectively in bunkhouses, saving money to send back to their families. Canada's first gurdwara (the Sikh place of worship) was established in a Vancouver house rented by the Khalsa Diwan Society. This temporary space catered to the spiritual needs of Sikhs—and it was free from British control.

All over British India, and in other colonies in Asia, the British controlled Sikh religious places with the cooperation of Sikh religious leaders. Many self-defined orthodox Sikhs worried that Sikhs were at the risk of being assimilated into the Hindu fold. The boundaries between Sikhs and Hindus were, in fact, quite porous; some Hindu families raised their eldest son as a Sikh to honour the historic sacrifices made by Sikhs in standing up to the tyranny of Mughal rulers. However, since 1857, the British had sought to define each Indian religious community in legal terms, disrupting identities that were complex and composite in aid of Britain's divide and rule policy.

Until 1904, Sikhs were listed as a subcategory under Hindus in the British Indian Army.[8] However, once being Sikh was accepted as an official religious identity, the British Indian Army emerged as a potent force in Sikhism's reinvigoration and renewal. Sikh baptismal ceremonies, morning prayers and other rites were made mandatory for anyone wishing to join the army. And all enlisted men had to adhere to the visible symbols of the Sikh faith, the Five K's—*kesh, kangha, kara, kirpan* and *kachera.*[9]

Two of the young men designated as *granthis* (those appointed to lead the reading of Sikh scriptures) of the new Sikh temple, Balwant Singh and Bhag Singh, were veterans of the British Indian Army. Bhag Singh was an excellent horseman, having served for five years in the iconic cavalry regiment the Tenth Bengal Lancers. Balwant Singh had been a member of another celebrated unit, the Thirty-sixth Sikh Infantry, twenty-one soldiers of which had dispelled British anxieties about Sikh loyalty in 1897 by fighting heroically to the last man rather than give up their strategic post during the Battle of Saragarhi near Afghanistan.[10] Both men considered themselves proud and equal British subjects, and they were prepared to push the king-emperor, Edward VII, to treat them as such.

The Vancouver gurdwara was not merely a place of communal worship for Sikhs. It served as a community centre for all South Asians, and so it was a natural place for British Columbia's South Asians to start organizing for their rights. They were supported in their efforts by highly educated and well-travelled South Asian activists, among them men from the eastern Indian coast province of Bengal and Punjabi intellectuals who had settled in the United States. Some of these émigrés spent time in Vancouver with the local leadership, extolling them to rise above their Sikh religious identity and the separatism encouraged by the British. The intensification of Indian migration to Canada coincided with a time of great political upheaval in British India, and many activists were using their freedom abroad to call for an end

RIGHT A Sikh procession in Vancouver. Two men carry *dhols,* traditional double-sided drums; two others have *khartaals,* traditional castanets. The boy seems to be playing the *manjira,* brass cymbals. The man third from front left sports the distinctive circular turban badge of the Forty-fifth (Rattray's) Sikhs, a British Indian Army regiment.

to British rule. They made the persuasive argument that South Asians would never be treated as equals while their homeland was subjugated by the British.

Chinese and Japanese residents of Canada, except for the rare few born in the country, had been stripped of their voting rights in 1885 and 1895 respectively. The situation of South Asians was different. As British subjects, South Asians needed only to prove they had resided for two years in Canada to be allowed to vote. In 1907, however, the wording in Section 7 of British Columbia's Provincial Elections Act was changed to read: "No Chinaman, Japanese, Hindu or Indian shall have his name placed on the register of voters for an electoral district, or be entitled to vote at any election." Since federal voting lists were based on provincial ones, South Asians lost the right to vote in federal elections at the same time. Like the Chinese and the Japanese, they became non-citizens, and, in a legal sense, aliens. The loss was significant. The right to vote was the defining mark of Canadian citizenship, so South Asians could no longer join the list of professions for which holding citizenship was a prerequisite.

On September 4, 1907, a race riot broke out in the U.S. border city of Bellingham, Washington. A mob of white workers—stirred up by the Asiatic Exclusion League, which had formed with the aim of keeping "Oriental" immigrants out of the United States—attacked and drove out over 250 South Asian men working in the lumber mills. The mayor offered shelter to a group of terrified men in the basement of Bellingham's city hall. Over the next few days, South Asians in the neighbouring states of Oregon and California were also targeted. Soon roughly seven hundred South Asian men, homeless and largely penniless, had crossed the border into Canada, seeking refuge in British territory.[11] Municipal authorities in Vancouver found them temporary housing, but issued pleas to the federal government for financial help and used the event to argue yet again that Canada must stop South Asian immigration. Laurier maintained his silence, worried his Liberal Party would lose seats in British Columbia if he took a stand.

A few thousand Asian immigrants had landed in Vancouver in the first seven months of 1907. The British Columbia government had once again been foiled by the federal government in its efforts to pass legislation based on the Natal Dictation Test. In early September, Vancouver newspapers claimed that the CP ship *Monteagle* was soon to land in the city's harbour carrying nearly two thousand South Asian, Chinese and Japanese immigrants. The reports fuelled public hysteria, and the Vancouver chapter of the Asiatic Exclusion League called for a mass demonstration.

HINDOO RELIGIOUS PROCESSION VANCOUVER B.C.

The league enjoyed widespread support; its membership included several municipal, provincial and federal politicians, including the mayor of Vancouver, Alexander Bethune.[12] More than ten thousand people showed up, and police allowed the mob to move towards the Japanese and Chinese quarters of Vancouver, even though their violent intentions were clear. The demonstrators marched to an anonymously penned anthem called "White Canada Forever."

Then let us stand united all
And show our father's might,
That won the home we call our own,
For white man's land we fight.
To Oriental grasp and greed
We'll surrender, no never.
Our watchword be God Save the King
White Canada Forever.[13]

ABOVE South Asian workers huddle in the basement of Bellingham's city hall, where the mayor of the city offered them shelter after the anti-Hindu riots of 1907. The September 1907 riots, sparked by Bellingham's Asiatic Exclusion League, set the stage for the Vancouver riot a few days later.

RIGHT South Asians wait at the Bellingham station in September 1907 for a train to take them north to Vancouver. They were seeking refuge as British subjects in the British territory of the Dominion of Canada.

THE WORM THAT TURNED

ACCORDING TO REPORTS THE VANCOUVER MOB WENT THROUGH THE CHINESE QUARTER LIKE THIS

BANZAI!

THEN RETURNED THROUGH THE JAPANESE QUARTER LIKE THIS

IMPERIAL CONSULATE GENERAL
OF JAPAN.
FOR THE DOMINION OF CANADA.

128808

385 LAURIER AVENUE EAST,

OTTAWA,_____190

Telegraphic message from Mr K.Ishie, at Vancouver B.C.

September. 8th, 1907.

Having arrived at Vancouver at 11 P.M. the 7th of September I have found that during the early part of the evening there was held a demonstration of the Anti-Japanese and Corean League, and at about 9 P.M. a number of rowdies, numbering from fifty to sixty, marched to the section of the city, where there are stores, kept by both the Japanese and Chinese, throwing stones at them, breaking glasses. Soon after this attack there came another one, this time the number, increasing to about five hundred, breaking all the glasses MMM of the front of the stores. So far only but one Japanese is said to ~~have been~~ MMMMM wounded. The city police force is said to be doing their best, but there is hardly any hope of relying upon their protection. Consul Mr Morikawa is staying at the seat of the disturbance, trying to press upon the City Police to extend their protection over the Japanese residents, and at the mean time to suppress the utmost excitement of the Japanese. There might be no further disturbance.

LEFT This telegram from the Japanese consul in Vancouver to Canadian prime minister Wilfrid Laurier describes the impact of the Vancouver riot on the Japanese community. The Asiatic Exclusion League was also known as the Japanese and Korean Exclusion League in the United States.

ABOVE In spite of its racist caricatures, this editorial cartoon from September 13, 1907, distills what happened during the Vancouver riots. The mob led by the Asiatic Exclusion League rampaged through Chinatown while the police stood by. In the Japanese section, the mob met fierce and sustained resistance and had to flee.

By the time the mob was finished in Chinatown, scores of Chinese-owned shops had been vandalized. Vancouver's Japanese community fared slightly better, since residents had quickly organized themselves and were ready to fight back in the streets. The riot continued until three in the morning, and daybreak revealed widespread devastation. The day after the riot there was a run on handguns all over Vancouver; traumatized, Japanese and Chinese men bought the weapons wherever they could find them. Others hired armed guards to protect their businesses and families.

ABOVE South Asian immigrants disembark from the *Monteagle* in Vancouver, 1907. Scores of passengers can also be seen in the background, near the stern of the ship. The ship arrived in the aftermath of the Vancouver riot, and protests led by the Asiatic Exclusion League had forced the immigrants to stay on the ship for a few days before landing.

RIGHT William Lyon Mackenzie King, as Canada's deputy minister of labour, was dispatched by the prime minister to look into the aftermath of the Vancouver riot. King would go on to become federal minister of labour and then Canada's longest-serving prime minister.

ON SEPTEMBER 11, four days after the Vancouver riot, the *Monteagle* arrived carrying a little more than half the anticipated number of Asians—901 South Asians, 149 Chinese and 115 Japanese. A small mob gathered on the pier and managed to block the immigrants from disembarking, and the authorities did little to curtail this vigilante action. The situation was so acute that the ship was rerouted to Victoria, where the Japanese passengers were allowed to land. The *Monteagle* returned to Vancouver the same day, but the South Asian passengers were again refused landing. Mayor Bethune himself donated $100 towards a fund to ship the South Asian passengers to Ottawa "with compliments."[14] Two days later, the South Asians and the Chinese were allowed to disembark without any trouble. But the violence and its aftermath finally drove home the message to Ottawa: Canada must remain a white man's country.

Laurier immediately set up a Royal Commission and appointed his protegé, William Lyon Mackenzie King, to head the investigation. King, in his early thirties at the time, held the post of deputy minister for labour. As the Asian sections of Vancouver braced for more possible attacks, King began to look into redress.

King was concerned mostly about the Japanese. The Vancouver riot threatened to mar the relationship between imperial Japan and Canada and would likely draw in Britain as well. King's files indicate the lengths to which Canada was willing to go

to make amends with a major trading partner and an imperial ally; they are also a haunting record of the trauma suffered by the victims. King and his team walked through Vancouver's Japanese neighbourhood precisely noting and diligently photographing the damage, urging victims to submit their claims. Shock mixed with defiance and dignity is seen in image after image of families standing next to their damaged properties.

King also held meetings with the Chinese community through the Chinese Board of Trade, though the commission did not undertake door-to-door written or photographic records in Chinatown. Ultimately, the Japanese and Chinese claims were compensated, on the understanding that no further legal action would be taken.

Once the claims for damages from the riot were settled, the Canadian government moved swiftly to stem the flow of immigrants from Asia. In November 1907, Laurier dispatched Rodolphe Lemieux, his minister of labour, to Japan to hold talks about controlling immigration. The result was a secret accord, a "gentlemen's agreement" in which Japan agreed to issue only four hundred passports a year to those wishing to migrate to Canada.

Later that fall, the prime minister requested that King to go to London to meet with the British authorities. The British Indian government had warned about the repercussions of Canada passing explicitly racist legislation, and imperial authorities in London had echoed those views. On his return, however, King stated in his report that the British were sympathetic to Canadian concerns: "That Canada should remain a white man's country is believed to not only be desirable for economic and social reasons, but highly necessary on political and national grounds."[15]

THE ARRIVAL OF twenty-eight-year-old William Hopkinson in Vancouver in the fall of 1907 signalled a new phase in the development of Canada's whites-only policy. Hopkinson had been born in Delhi, and historian Hugh Johnston speculates that

C 33100

✓

INCIDENT No 25

re/RIOT at City of Vancouver,
B. C., and Claim for damages
to property of Japanese
Residents.

LOCATION, No. 453 STREET, Powell

NAME, Hori Jenga BUSINESS,

NATURE & PARTICULARS OF DAMAGE DONE Sept 7, 1907.

(1) 3'6" x 5'0" .... $ 12.00

.... $

.... $

.... $

.... $

.... $

LENGTH OF TIME OF BUSINESS SUSPENSION-- $ 12.00

6 days Approximate Loss $

REMARKS:

PHOTOGRAPH OF PREMISES AT TIME OF

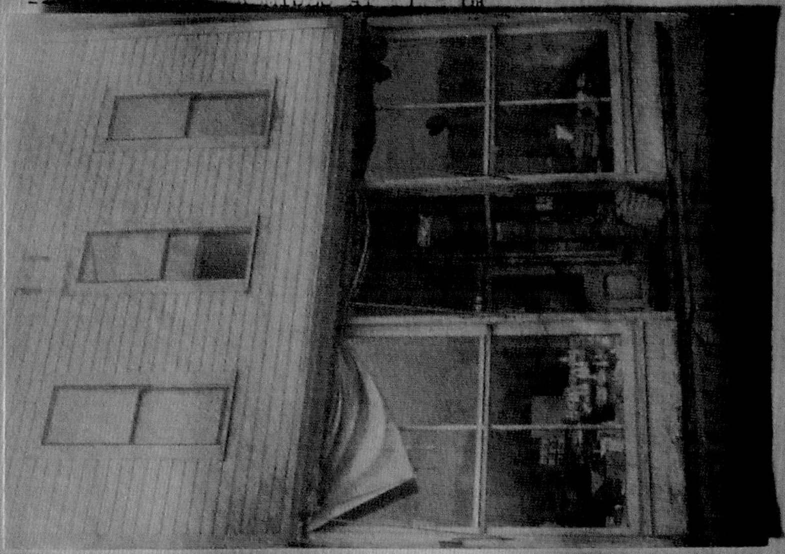

.... CLAIMANT.

.... ARCHITECT & ASSESSOR.

WITNESS: A Nicholls 19th September 1907.

FAR LEFT King produced a meticulously documented and illustrated report showing the damage caused to Japanese-owned homes and businesses by the Vancouver rioters.

TOP LEFT These cyanotype prints, with their typical blue tint, were made from photographs taken by King or an assisting photographer. They include the people who live or work in each building, and so document not only the property damage but also the shock and trauma caused by the violence.

BOTTOM LEFT A Sikh bystander can be seen at the extreme right. While South Asians were not targeted in the violence, the government's response—which included restricting immigration from British India—directly impacted them.

RIGHT Soon after the Vancouver riot, Canada sought to restrict Japanese immigration. Japan entered into a face-saving secret accord, a "gentlemen's agreement" in which it agreed to issue only four hundred passports a year to those wishing to migrate to Canada.

BELOW Boarded-up storefronts in Chinatown. Imperial Japan was a strong ally, but China was not as important to Canadian interests, so King did not prepare as detailed of a report on Chinese losses. He did, however, ensure that all claims were settled to everyone's satisfaction.

Hopkinson's mother may have been of mixed Indian and European heritage.[16] His British father, an army officer, had been killed in action in Afghanistan. Hopkinson had served for four years as an inspector with the Calcutta police and had also been attached to the Department of Criminal Intelligence (DCI) of the British Indian government. His activities in Canada indicate that he never stopped working for British intelligence in India, but the reasons for his move to Vancouver remain mysterious.

Hopkinson almost immediately showed his ability to use the media to further the Imperial agenda. He encouraged a British correspondent for the *Times* of London to publish a story about seditious activity aimed at the armed overthrow of British rule in India being fomented by activists in Vancouver and Seattle. Hopkinson's fluency in Hindustani and, he claimed, in Punjabi, made him an invaluable resource for Canadian immigration officers, who hired him as an interpreter. His influence gained him an interview with William Lyon Mackenzie King, who by the spring of 1908 was engaged in developing a strategy for the federal government on how to deal with the "Hindus."

In his recommendations to the Laurier government as deputy minister of labour, Mackenzie King repeated, and indeed appropriated, some of the earliest objections to immigrants from British India, writing that they were "inassimilable" and that "the climate of the country was not suited to the Hindu ... The experience has shown that immigrants of this class having been accustomed to the conditions of a tropical climate are wholly unsuited to this country and their inability to readily adapt themselves to their surroundings so entirely different inevitably brings upon them much suffering and privation."[17] King alerted Ottawa that another reason for blocking South Asian immigration would be to undermine any seditious and treasonous activity taking place on Canadian soil. Race, immigration, empire and security were now explicitly tied together.

After analyzing the situation, King devised an original and clever plan: he came up with two orders-in-council to be added to the Immigration Act of 1906. Under the Canadian parliamentary system, an order-in-council is a regulation that can be added to existing legislation. The first order-in-council stated: "All immigrants must come to Canada via a through ticket and by continuous journey from their country of birth or citizenship." The second read as follows: "All immigrants from Asia must have in their possession $200."

At issue was the very successful shipping line that Canadian Pacific ran between Calcutta, then the capital of India, and Vancouver. From the outset, King agreed

REPORT

BY

W. L. MACKENZIE KING, C.M.G., DEPUTY MINISTER OF LABOUR, ON HIS MISSION TO ENGLAND TO CONFER WITH THE BRITISH AUTHORITIES ON THE SUBJECT OF IMMIGRATION TO CANADA FROM THE ORIENT, AND IMMIGRATION FROM INDIA IN PARTICULAR.

To His Excellency the Governor General in Council:

I have the honour to submit to Your Excellency in Council, a report on my mission to Great Britain to confer with the British authorities on the subject of immigration from the Orient, and immigration from India in particular, the circumstances and objects of which mission are briefly detailed in the following copy of a report of the Committee of the Privy Council, approved by His Excellency the Governor General on March 2, 1908:—

'On a memorandum dated 2nd March, 1908, from the Right Honourable Sir Wilfrid Laurier, representing that notwithstanding the regulations for the restriction of immigration from the Orient, certain classes of immigrants, in particular British East Indians, are being induced to come to Canada under circumstances which may necessitate a refusal of their admission to our shores;

'That experience has shown that immigrants of this class, having been accustomed to the conditions of a tropical climate, are wholly unsuited to this country, and that their inability to readily adapt themselves to surroundings so entirely different inevitably brings upon them much suffering and privation; also, that were such immigration allowed to reach any considerable dimensions, it would result in a serious disturbance to industrial and economic conditions in portions of the Dominion, and especially in the province of British Columbia;

'That an effective restriction of immigration from India is desirable, therefore, not less in the interest of the East Indians themselves, than in the interest of the Canadian people;

'That moreover, the whole subject of Oriental immigration is one of first concern to Canada, and affecting, as it does, the relations of the Dominion with foreign powers, and the relations of our people with fellow British subjects in India, involves considerations of the highest importance, not only to Canada, but to the British Empire as a whole;

'That it is desirable that on this important question there should be as complete an interchange of views between the authorities of Great Britain and Canada as may be possible, and that in reference to it there should be a complete understanding between the governments of the two countries;

'Mr. W. L. Mackenzie King, C.M.G., Deputy Minister of Labour, has recently made full enquiry under Royal Commission into the causes by which

*** P.C.1255. 1

AT THE GOVERNMENT HOUSE AT OTTAWA;

Wednesday the 3rd day of June, 1908:

PRESENT:

HIS EXCELLENCY

THE GOVERNOR GENERAL IN COUNCIL:

WHEREAS by the Order in Council of the 8th January 1908 it is provided that in accordance with section 20 of the Immigration Act the Immigration Agent at any port shall require every immigrant, male or female, eighteen years of age or over, to have in his or her possession money to a minimum amount of twenty-five dollars, in addition to a ticket to his or her destination in Canada, unless satisfactory evidence is furnished that the immigrant is going to some definite employment or to relatives or friends already settled in Canada, who will take care of such immigrant, and by a further Order in Council of the 27th March, 1908, this arrangement is continued in force;

AND WHEREAS Canada is looking primarily for immigrants of an agricultural class to occupy vacant lands, and as immigrants from Asia belong as a rule to labouring classes, and their language and mode of life render them unsuited for settlement in Canada where there are no colonies of their own people to ensure their maintenance in case of their inability to secure employment, it is necessary that provision be made so that such immigrants

may

In duplicate to Gov. Genl 4 June 08 — Ackgd 17 June 1908
to High Commissioner 4 " "
In duplicate to Secretary 4 " "
to Governor General 9 " "
Canada Gazette page 3276 - 20/6/08

with a perception common in Vancouver, and one shared by the immigration department, that shipping company agents were enticing people in the Punjab to buy tickets to Canada. Implicit in the charge was the accusation that Canadian Pacific was more concerned about its profits than about protecting the national character—in essence the "whiteness"—of Canada.

The Canadian government first put pressure on CP to stop selling tickets to Indians. When that did not entirely stem the flow, the government forced the company to end the direct voyages. One concern, though, was that the continuous journey regulation might be applied universally, since it came into effect just as immigration from Europe was starting to peak. Many European immigrants, such as those from eastern and central Europe, could not come to Canada via continuous journey; many had to travel first to ports in other countries and then catch a ship to Canada from there. If immigration officers were to enforce the continuous journey regulation and apply it to European immigrants, tens of thousands of "desirable" people would be barred from entering the country. This did happen in a few cases; for example, two Europeans, a Russian and a Frenchman, arrived in Canada via Japan. They were denied entry by zealous Canadian immigration officers, but were gladly accepted into the United States.[18] Superintendent of Immigration W.D. Scott composed a confidential memo clarifying the government's intent: "Please bear in mind that the newly issued Order-in-Council re: 'continuous journey' is absolutely prohibitive in its terms but that it is only intended to enforce it strictly against really undesirable immigrants. You will understand, therefore, that a great deal is left to your own discretion with regards to the application of that particular Order."[19]

While Scott felt the need to underscore the intent of the continuous journey regulation for immigration officials, it was an open secret in the public sphere that the measure was aimed at people from British India. The continuous journey regulation and its application provided a fascinating example of how official intent, which reflected the popular attitudes of the day, could be hidden in the wording of a

LEFT Canada used legislation to restrict Chinese immigrants, regulations to exclude South Asians and a secret agreement to limit Japanese immigration. Combined, these measures amounted to a White Canada immigration policy—but unlike Australia, Canada did not officially name it.

ABOVE This so-called "In the Pocket" order-in-council, dated June 3, 1908, was signed by Prime Minister Wilfrid Laurier and then submitted to Governor General Grey for approval. Like the continuous journey regulation, this new regulation targeted South Asians, who now had to prove that they had $200 with them on arrival in Canada.

TOP RIGHT An aboriginal family on a wharf in Vancouver, 1903. The creation of "White Canada" included a concerted push to "civilize the Indian" by setting up residential schools and outlawing traditional ceremonies.

BOTTOM RIGHT No details are available about this image from 1905, in which a group of settlers in Saskatoon, Saskatchewan, pose behind an aboriginal man. Treaties resulted in the dispossession and displacement of First Nations people from their homelands onto reserves. The resulting Crown land was offered free to European immigrants, who could then set up homesteads.

seemingly universal law, the application of which was backed by a secret handshake among all levels of government, from the immigration officer on the ground right up to the prime minister.

The second order-in-council was clearly discriminatory, since white immigrants were required to have only $25 in their possession upon arrival in Canada. Asians were now required to have eight times that amount. This requirement did not apply to those covered by a treaty, such as the Japanese; nor did it apply to the Chinese, who were already covered by Canada's head tax. The amount was not only a small fortune for people coming from British India, but nearly half a year's salary for the average Canadian worker.[20]

Unlike the Chinese and Japanese governments, who were willing to at least protest when discriminatory measures against their citizens were imposed, the government of India was perfectly satisfied with the new measures. In a letter to Wilfrid Laurier on March 1, 1909, Lord Minto, Viceroy of India, wrote: "We hold the view that the continuous passage and the two hundred dollar regulations are likely to prove effective in putting a stop to immigration of Indian labour. We have published the conditions imposed by Canada widely... We raise no objections to the methods adopted by Canada, and we have not any intention to raising questions [*sic*] regarding them."[21]

The numbers speak for themselves about the effectiveness of the continuous journey regulation and the zeal with which it was applied. In 1907–8, 2,623 Indian immigrants were allowed to enter Canada; in 1908–9, the number plunged to 6. In 1909–10, only 10 were admitted, and in 1910–11 only 5.[22] The provision also kept out Japanese immigrants who were bypassing the gentlemen's agreement between Britain and Japan by going first to Hawaii. Hence, although Canada did not have a singularly defined White Canada policy, the government of the time pursued its idea of nation by imposing a variety of measures, largely defined by imperial politics, to create a population that was overwhelmingly of European descent.

Canada's aboriginal peoples were kept strictly on the margins. Residential schools that sought to "civilize" aboriginal children, legal restrictions on traditional aboriginal practices, externally applied rules that defined who was an Indian, and the encroachment on and confiscation of traditional lands were deliberate policies designed to destroy aboriginal culture and ways of living. The Indians were seen by government as a vanishing race, and those who survived would be assimilated into European Canadian culture, thus solving the "Indian problem."

Photographed by Elgin & Shepard, Minneapolis

A TRAIN OF AMERICAN IMMIGRANTS INTO CANADA

Photographed by Steele & Co., Winnipeg

COWBOYS RAFTING ON THE LITTLE BOW RIVER AT A GENERAL "ROUND UP"

This primitive method of transportation is being rapidly supplanted by the railroads

Photographed by Mathers

FREIGHT LEAVING EDMONTON FOR LLOYDMINSTER

Settlers going into new homes in western Canada by way of the Saskatchewan River

The continuous journey regulation led to the near-absolute barring of South Asians from Canada in ways the explicitly exclusionary Chinese Immigration Act of 1923 did not. Although the regulation was initially defeated by the courts, the federal government moved quickly to close the loopholes.

Frank Oliver, Canada's minister of the interior, was required to put the regulation up for debate in Parliament before it could be added to the Immigration Act. R.G. MacPherson, the Liberal MP from Vancouver, came to the minister's defence, engaging in a great display of verbal gymnastics to deny that the regulation targeted "Hindus," as Conservative Party MP Sam Hughes accused. Hughes, the Conservative MP for Victoria North, was eager to corner MacPherson and make him admit the unstated objective of the regulation, which MacPherson finally did: "Yes, to exclude Hindus and Asiatics and all kinds of undesirable people."[23]

ST PAUL-MINNEAPOLIS DULUTH, SUPERIOR to ESTEVAN WEYBURN MOOSE JAW $12.00

The Opposition's objections were based entirely on a perceived lack of due process, however. When the ruling Liberals went on the offensive, Opposition MPs were quick to backtrack, lest anyone think that the Conservative Party had become a proponent of open immigration. Sam Hughes voiced the contradictory yearnings of Canadians: "I want to put myself on record, I am in favour of a white man's country but also in favour of a decent country."[24] Once consensus about the racial homogeneity of Canada had been restored, Parliament moved on to more pressing matters.

IN THE FALL of 1908, immigration officials came up with a plan for the mass relocation of the South Asians who had settled in Canada. If the official argument was that "Hindus were not suited for the climate of Canada," then it followed they would be better off in a British territory with a warmer climate. The closest such territory was British Honduras (now Belize), nestled in the thin neck of Central America along the Atlantic coast. It speaks to the self-confidence of Vancouver's South Asian community, and to its members' awareness of their rights, that they organized in the

LEFT Encouraged by the Canadian government, hundreds of thousands of Euro-American immigrants came north on trains dubbed "prairie schooners" to settle in the Canadian West. This massive movement of people, referred to as "the American invasion," was welcomed, unlike the "Hindu invasion" that was happening at the same time.

ABOVE Recognizing that much of the American West had already been settled, Canadian immigration officials enticed white American settlers to Canada.

ABOVE Just over a thousand African Americans were allowed into Canada during the period in which more than a million Euro-Americans settled the Canadian West. The same argument used to block South Asians was used against African Americans—the climate of Canada was deemed unsuitable for them.

RIGHT Firewood delivery man Kartar Singh, early 1900s. Stripped of their right to vote, South Asians were barred from a vast range of professions and were compelled to find work as labourers or set up small businesses. Fuel delivery became an important niche for South Asian businessmen.

ABOVE A photo postcard shows two Sikh men out for a stroll in New Westminster, a suburb of Vancouver. The man on the left is wearing his ceremonial army jacket with white piping.

RIGHT A well-dressed Sikh gentleman with rolled umbrella in hand strides through downtown Vancouver. South Asian men were not allowed to bring their wives and children into Canada, in order to discourage permanent settlement.

LEFT South Asians were relegated to low-paying jobs after they were stripped of their right to vote in 1907. They were also paid less than white workers, yet many South Asians still managed to make enough money to support their families back home in British India.

BELOW This unusual image shows two men poised for traditional *kushti*, a wrestling match. Very little was recorded about the recreational pastimes of B.C.'s early South Asian community.

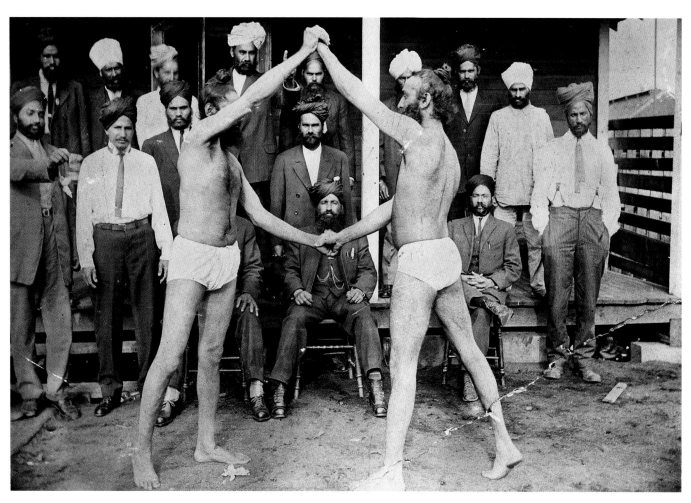

newly inaugurated gurdwara on Second Avenue. In the face of bureaucratic intimidation and threats of deportation, they roundly rejected the British Honduras plan. William Hopkinson had been central to the relocation initiative, and he was now deeply resented by many in the community.

Two months later, the Dominion government invited the governor of British Honduras, Colonel E.J.E. Swayne, to Ottawa. Swayne, a self-described "old India officer," had served in the British Indian Army, leading troops in military campaigns on the Afghan frontier and in northern Africa. Swayne was sympathetic to Canadian concerns, but he was also aware that the demographics of the Indian community in Vancouver would require delicate handling for the preservation of the empire. After a visit to Vancouver, he noted with some anxiety in a confidential memo: "They have coalesced from the common need of protection against the hostility of white labour, and Punjabi-Mohamedans [*sic*], Sikhs, and Hindus from the Punjab, and Brahmins from the N.W. and from lower Bengal, have been brought together in a way that could not have happened in India."[25] Swayne pointed out that, in addition to the nationalists in their midst, South Asian immigrants were being exposed to public

lectures by American socialists such as Emma Goldman, who had recently spoken in Vancouver, and as a result could infect others with "ill digested socialist ideas" that could also spread to India.

Swayne was instrumental in suggesting that William Hopkinson be hired as a Dominion police officer.[26] His recommendation was immediately accepted, and Hopkinson was also appointed as an immigration inspector. It was understood that in his dual role he would keep a close watch on South Asian activity in Vancouver. He would go on to single-handedly build a network of informants throughout South Asian communities. Hopkinson would also cultivate a relationship with American authorities and hence be able to monitor the entire Pacific coast.

Another influential figure who understood the larger imperial picture was Canada's governor general, Lord Earl Grey. Like his counterpart in India, Lord Minto (the viceroy, who was also Grey's predecessor as Canada's governor general), Lord Grey was acutely aware of the dangers to British rule in India that lurked in Canada, dangers most Canadians failed to appreciate. Through direct contact with William Hopkinson, Grey kept an eye on South Asian nationalists in Vancouver.

Hopkinson became an irreplaceable agent for British imperial intelligence in North America. Considerable power and responsibility rested on the shoulders of this ambitious young man. His targets in the South Asian community were for the most part also young men, emboldened by their exposure to the relative freedoms of

LEFT The honourable discharge certificate was prized not only by veterans like Bhagwan Singh, but also by their descendants. Regiments looked favourably upon recruiting men from the same family. If the younger men met the criteria, they were recruited into the same regiments as their elders.

RECOMMENDATION FOR CIVIL EMPLOYMENT.
(See A. R. I., Vol. II para 457.)

I. A. F. Y1962.

The bearer ~~reservist~~ pensioner No. *3364* Rank *Naick* Name *Bhagwan Singh*

late of the *Guide Infy.*, resident in the village of *Akalgarh* Tehsil *Ludhiana* District *Ludhiana* is desirous of obtaining employment as a *Orderly Jemadar in Tehsil*, and it is hoped his application will receive favourable consideration. *The lowest salary he would accept is (a) R 12/- at or near his home; or (b) Rs 15/- away from his home.*

He has served for *21* years *26/31* months, his character has been *Exemplary* and he is in possession of *1* medals and *2* clasps. He is ———— intelligent.

QUALIFICATIONS.

1. Languages *Panjabi*
2. Reading and writing *Gurmukhi*
3. Arithmetic *no*
4. Trade *Zamindar*

5. General health *fine*
6. If strong, active and energetic *Yes*
7. Whether fit for out or } in-door work } *fit for either*

N. B.—Any employer engaging the applicant is requested to kindly inform the Recruiting Staff Officer of the class concerned, see para 62s. A. R. I., Vol. II) at* *Jullundur* or if the man resides in the Madras Command the officer in charge of pensioners at the station at which he draws his pension, of the date, nature, and salary of appointment.

Note—The individual will be given a copy, and another sent to the R. S. O. of the class concerned, or Superintendent of Pensions, Madras, through, in the case of a pensioner in the Madras Command, the pension paymaster of station of residence.

Station *Mardan*

Date *9. 11. 1907*

*To be filled in by O. C.

for Comdg. *Major*
O. C. Corps of Guides

ABOVE A certificate recommending veteran Bhagwan Singh for civil employment, dated 1907. In 1909, as a response to growing discrimination, a number of veterans of the British Indian Army gathered in Vancouver to burn their uniforms and documents of service. This event was disquieting enough to be reported to imperial authorities in British India.

North America to behave in ways few would dare in India. Hopkinson was unfazed by the loathing his presence generated in some parts of the community, knowing there were many South Asian immigrants who remained loyal to the Crown and were willing to serve as informants.

Lohri is a traditional bonfire that marks midwinter in Punjab, and on October 3, 1909, an unusual *lohri*-like bonfire was lit on the grounds of the Vancouver gurdwara. Natha Singh, a British Indian Army veteran, brought forward an extraordinary motion to the gathered assembly: "Our uniforms and medals show that we have fought for the British as mercenaries against our own countrymen and to enslave other Asian nations. The uniforms and medals are the symbols of our slavery. I propose that no member of the executive of the Sikh Temple should wear any kind of medals, buttons, uniforms or insignias which may signify that the position of the party wearing the article is nothing but a slave to British supremacy."[27] Once the motion was seconded and carried, Natha Singh was joined by other Sikh, Hindu and Muslim veterans in throwing their uniforms, discharge certificates and photographs into the fire. These artifacts were normally passed from father to son and served to assist the next generation in enlisting. By burning these items, the men knew they were irrevocably severing their ties with the Crown.

This non-violent act was full of portent. Alerted by his informants, Hopkinson sent off a detailed report on the gathering, ringing alarm bells in London and Calcutta. The Great Uprising of 1857 was still within living memory, and Britain's fears about the loyalty of the "native" troops had never really abated.[28] The slightest whiff of disloyalty in anyone remotely connected to "the sword arm of the British Empire" was considered a serious threat to the imperial order.

On January 14, 1910, a South Asian man named Husain Rahim landed in Vancouver claiming he was en route to New York, with further plans to travel to England via Montreal. Since he arrived as a tourist, the continuous journey regulation did not apply. And perhaps immigration officials let him in on their discretion, since he was a moustachioed, westernized South Asian who not only spoke and wrote excellent English, but also had a first-class train ticket booked to Montreal.

William Hopkinson did not see Husain Rahim in that light. He claimed that Rahim was not a Muslim but in fact a Hindu by the name of Chagan Khairaj Varma, born and raised in Porbandar in Gujarat, India. Hopkinson alleged that Rahim had taken on the new Muslim name in Honolulu, where he had supposedly gone after leaving Japan under a cloud of suspicion over financial matters.

A few months after his arrival, Rahim returned from eastern Canada to Vancouver, where he incorporated a real estate company, the Canada India Supply & Trust Company, and established himself quickly in the community. When Hopkinson alerted his superiors that Rahim was not a tourist but had entered Canada in contravention of the continuous journey regulation, Rahim was arrested. Community members rallied around him and posted bail. However, immigration officers discovered that Rahim's notebook included not only a detailed formula for making nitroglycerine but the names and addresses of Indian nationalists from all over Europe, the United States and Africa. A report submitted to Ottawa, London

ABOVE Husain Rahim, businessman, realtor, publisher of the *Hindustanee*, president of the United India League and member of the Socialist Party of Canada. Rahim was one of the leaders of the Shore Committee that sought to help the *Komagata Maru* passengers.

and Calcutta stated, "Rahim was most indignant at the time of his arrest attempting to stand off our Inspector Hopkinson amongst other things making remarks to the effect: 'You drive us Hindus out of Canada and we will drive every white man out of India.'"[29]

Rahim's deportation case was thrown out when the court ruled that immigration officers had not followed due process. An alarmed Hopkinson wrote his supervisors in Ottawa:

> The failure … of the Department to deport Rahim from Canada has so bolstered up his position in the Hindu community here as to make him a leader and a counselor in respect to all matters concerning their community … Canada would be well rid of Rahim and the exposure of his true character would have a very beneficial effect on [the] community.[30]

Rahim would indeed become an important community leader. In 1910, he joined the nascent United India League, and along with Balwant Singh and Bhag Singh established a special South Asian chapter of the Vancouver-based Socialist Party of Canada.

The June 5, 1910, edition of the *New York Times* asserted that a revolution was brewing in Vancouver; the community's simmering anger was being tapped by seditionists who were collecting money to buy arms in British India.[31] It is likely that Indian nationalists in Vancouver were also affected by nationalist fervour in the local Chinese community. Chinese revolutionary leader Dr. Sun Yat-sen had made several visits to Vancouver to raise awareness and funds; the goal was to overthrow the imperial rulers of China and replace them with a democratic republic. Many in Vancouver's Chinese community believed that a stronger China would in turn lead to better treatment of the Chinese abroad, a belief the South Asian community shared vis-à-vis their own position in Canada. Both communities witnessed the fanfare accorded the Imperial Japanese Navy battleships that docked in Vancouver from time to time.

When Canada's Immigration Act was overhauled in 1910, the continuous journey regulation was included. The amended act now gave sweeping powers to the government to exclude people explicitly on the basis of race. Section 38 mentioned specifically immigrants "belonging to any race deemed unsuited to the climate or requirements of Canada." Section 41 of the new act, obviously drafted in response

LEFT Many South Asian activists were influenced by and supported by the Vancouver-based Socialist Party of Canada, which created a specific chapter for the community. The revolutionary Ghadar Party, formed south of the border, also incorporated much from socialist thought.

to nationalist organizing by South Asians and groups such as the Irish, also identified as undesirable any immigrant who "advocated in Canada the overthrow by force or violence of the government of Great Britain or Canada."[32] Minister of the Interior Frank Oliver offered the following justification: "We cannot tell at what time, or under what circumstances, there may be a sudden movement of people from one part of the world or another, and we want to be in a position to check it, should public policy demand such an action."[33]

With the White Canada policy now backed by stronger legislation, early in 1911 Balwant Singh and Bhag Singh decided to call attention to Canada's discriminatory laws by taking direct personal action. They returned to India—where both had left behind wives and children—to lecture publicly about the continuous journey regulation. When they tried to return with their families from Calcutta, they were refused tickets to Vancouver. After petitioning the viceroy of India to no avail, they continued lobbying from Hong Kong, again with no result. Around the same time, the Khalsa Diwan Society sent a delegation from Vancouver to Ottawa, among other things drawing attention to the loyalty of Sikhs to the British Crown since 1857.

In September 1911, Wilfrid Laurier and his Liberal Party lost the federal election to the Conservatives under Robert Borden. In Vancouver, an even more strident opponent of Asian immigration, H.H. Stevens, became the local member of Parliament. "The Hindus never did one solitary thing for humanity in the past two thousand years and will probably not in the next two thousand," Stevens had once declared.[34] A primary school teacher and local militia reservist named Malcolm Reid was appointed immigration inspector in charge of the Vancouver office. Reid owed his new job to Stevens, and he made sure to funnel all pertinent information about Asian, and particularly "Hindu," immigration to the newly elected M P.

Balwant Singh and Bhag Singh finally managed to buy tickets on the *Monteagle*, which was travelling from Hong Kong to San Francisco via Vancouver. But as soon as they disembarked, their wives and children were arrested and held in detention. The two men petitioned, and support was forthcoming from many allies, including the Quakers. Even the *Montreal Witness*, a Protestant newspaper, urged the government to let in the women and children, arguing that their arrest was "a miserable blot on the honour of Canada as a British nation, a denial of the most primary human rights, and a breach of Imperial loyalty."[35] Fearing the possible repercussions, H.H. Stevens counselled the federal government to allow the families to stay, and permission was granted to that effect in January 1912, as an act of grace, and without establishing a precedent.

ABOVE Soon after his coronation in 1911, King George V hands decorations to colonial and British Indian Army troops; the latter are seen just behind the canopy. Canadian and British Indian Army troops often encountered each other at imperial events.

A New Problem for Uncle Sam

ABOVE Anti-Asian sentiment was no less prevalent in the United States. To discourage the permanent settlement of South Asians, states like California passed anti-miscegenation laws to prevent non-whites from marrying white women.

Although the door remained firmly shut to South Asian immigrants, British, European and American immigration to Canada was reaching unprecedented levels. In 1913, more than 400,000 immigrants were admitted, the single largest influx of immigrants in any year to date.[36] However, the argument about the unsuitability of Canada's climate was used to block the flow of African Americans into the Canadian West. More than a million European Americans came north during the early 1900s; just over a thousand African Americans were let in.

Frustration grew among South Asian activists, and in early 1913 the Khalsa Diwan Society and the United India League sent a deputation led by Balwant Singh first to London, where British authorities predictably stonewalled them, and then to India.

That same year, the Hindustani Workers of the Pacific Coast, a revolutionary organization, crystallized south of the border in Astoria, Oregon. It would soon become known, after the title of its magazine, as the Ghadar Party—a provocative name, since *ghadar* means mutiny. The new party, from its headquarters in Stockton, California, advocated the armed overthrow of the British Empire, extolling Indian soldiers to mutiny once again. Its formation was the opening shot in what the British courts in India would dub a "war against the King Emperor." The Ghadarite vision was radical; they imagined a United States of India as a free, secular, inclusive democratic republic that embraced all religions and privileged none. William Hopkinson kept a wary eye on the group and knew that Husain Rahim, Bhag Singh, Balwant Singh and Sohan Lal, among others, were members.

Balwant Singh and his colleagues continued their lobbying efforts in India, holding public meetings and seeking face-to-face meetings with British officials, including the lieutenant governor of Punjab, Sir Michael O'Dwyer, who detailed the discussion in a subsequent memorandum to the viceroy. By this time, small groups of South Asians had started arriving in Victoria, British Columbia, having bought direct passage on Japanese ships from Calcutta. Fewer than fifty people managed to land, but the level of anxiety that the continuous journey regulation was failing, as expressed in the British Columbia press, bordered on paranoia.

ABOVE This photograph of two Sikh immigrants arriving in the U.S. from Hong Kong was taken in 1913 by Asahel Curtis, brother of the famed photographer Edward Curtis, who spent two decades documenting aboriginal peoples for his twenty-volume work *The North American Indian*.

LEFT South Asian men arrive in Seattle aboard the *Minnesota* in 1913. The U.S. gradually passed its own restrictive laws to put a stop to immigration from British India, and denied citizenship rights to South Asians for decades.

ABOVE Husain Rahim (*fourth from left*) with fellow activists in November 1913, in front of a detention facility in Victoria. Some of the thirty-nine Sikh detainees can be seen in the background. This rare image encapsulates the struggles against exclusion faced by the South Asian community.

On October 13, 1913, thirty-nine Sikhs arriving in Victoria via Hong Kong on a Japanese ship called the *Panama Maru* were promptly detained. Vancouver M P H.H. Stevens declared to the *Daily Province:* "The arrival of this party in Victoria is the result of a well organized and deliberate attempt to evade the regulation with the view to an extended influx of Hindus."[37]

The South Asian community, led by Husain Rahim, hired Vancouver lawyer J. Edward Bird. Bird opted for a test case: the verdict received by the selected man, Narain Singh, would be applicable to the remaining thirty-eight. His arguments sought to establish contradictions and errors in both orders-in-council. It was impossible to buy a direct ticket from Calcutta, hence the men had come via Hong Kong. The orders-in-council referred to native or naturalized citizens, but the Immigration Act used the term "citizen." The requirement for each person to have $200 did not specify that the money had to be in actual possession; rather, the person simply had to be able to prove he did have that much.

ਜਿਲਦ ਦੂਜੀ   ਨਵੰਬਰ ੫ ਸੰਮਤ ੧੬੧
VOL. 2   NOVEMBER 5 1913

ਦੁਖੀਆ ਦਰਦ ਘਾਲੇ ਦੇਪਲ ਜਾਲੇ ਤੂ ਪਨੀ

PLEAD FOR JUSTICE

THIRTY-NINE SIKHS IN CUSTODY AT VICTORIA, B.C

ਵਿਕ ਟੋਰੀਏ ਦੇ ਬੰਦੀ ਖਾਨੇ ਵਿਚ ਹੁਰੇ
ਹੋਏ ਉਨਤਾਲੀ ਸਿੰਘ

In *Rex vs. Thirty-nine Hindus,* Chief Justice Gordon Hunter declared the continuous journey regulation to be ultra vires—i.e., beyond the powers of the Immigration Act as set out in the constitution.[38] In agreeing with Bird, Chief Justice Hunter based his ruling on a strictly technical reading of the law. The South Asian men were allowed to land. It was an astonishing victory, and word spread around the world that, for now at least, Canada's door was open. This was what Stevens had feared, he told the *Daily Province.* "I have no doubt that the Dominion authorities are now aroused to a keen sense of the importance of the recent adverse… ruling by Chief Justice Hunter regarding the powers of immigration officials under the Orders-in-Council passed at Ottawa and will take up and grapple with the issue without delay and arrive at a satisfactory solution to the whole involved problem."[39] Canada did not appeal the decision, but revised orders-in-council were soon issued. It remained to be seen if they could withstand a legal challenge.

3 ──

THE KOMAGATA MARU
AT THE GATES OF CANADA

THE NEWS OF the pivotal decision by Chief Justice Hunter reached hundreds of would-be immigrants stranded in Asian ports. In March 1914, one group met with Gurdit Singh in the Hong Kong gurdwara.[1] A compact man in his mid-fifties, Singh was the antithesis of the rough Sikh farmer from the villages of Punjab. A keen sartorial sense kept him looking sharp; his greying beard, untrimmed in the orthodox Sikh style, added a dash of worldly wisdom. Although his roots lay in the village of Sarhali, near Amritsar, Gurdit Singh had been part of the early wave of migrants from Punjab. A quietly devout Sikh, he visited gurdwaras wherever he travelled. Settled in the Malay States for the previous few decades, he had amassed wealth and prestige as a government contractor whose dealings took him all over Southeast Asia. Government contracts required a knowledge of English, and cutting deals with local businessmen, suppliers and workers meant learning Malay—Gurdit was fluent.[2] Success in business also required a solid knowledge of the colonial system. Gurdit Singh had learned the importance of British jurisprudence, and he was known to be a litigious man.

In the spring of 1914, Gurdit was at a personal and professional crossroads, haunted by a feeling that he wanted to contribute to the welfare of his compatriots. In his sales pitch to potential passengers to Canada, he wrote:

When I came to Hong-Kong on some private business... I could not bear the grief and hardship of the Vancouver emigrants, who had been waiting in the Sikh temple. It was a matter of injustice and darkness, I thought, because our brethren were passing their days in a miserable state... while staying here for one year and spending money from their own pocket.[3]

Gurdit Singh was spurred into action by the Hunter decision, knowing he had to act before the window of opportunity closed. When he announced his intention of selling one-way tickets to Vancouver, a German shipping agent offered him the *Komagata Maru*, a former German ship recently acquired by a Japanese firm. Singh signed a charter and put the money towards a retrofit that would allow the freighter to carry passengers. By Singh's calculations, he needed five hundred passengers to make the voyage worthwhile, and including a cargo of 1,500 tons of coal would add to the profit margin.

Gurdit Singh sought an audience with Claud Severn, acting governor of Hong Kong, to inform the official of his plans. The two were acquainted, having both spent time in the Malay States. In his later memoir, *The Voyage of the Komagata Maru, or India's Slavery Abroad*, Singh claims he assured Severn: "But my object is purely commercial and economic and is no way political... This first trip is an experimental one. On my return from Canada, I will equip four ships, and take them from Calcutta to Canada... and a regular service would thus be commenced."[4] Severn, unable to dissuade Singh from mounting the voyage, issued last-minute orders for the police to hold the ship back, hoping his urgent telegram to Ottawa would result in a clear warning issued by Canada.

An indignant Gurdit Singh approached the lawyers of a leading British law firm in Hong Kong, who were unequivocal in their assessment: "We have to advise you that in our opinion there are no restrictions upon the immigration by Indians from the Colony."[5] For reasons unknown, there had been no immediate response from Ottawa, and Hong Kong authorities were no longer able to detain the *Komagata Maru*. Their tactics had managed to intimidate potential passengers, however, and many backed out.

Gurdit Singh was financially and contractually committed to the voyage. He asked the remaining passengers for additional funds and promised to pay them back in Vancouver. He was certain that he could pick up additional passengers in other Asian ports, too, and he was partially successful. Although the *Komagata Maru* departed from Hong Kong on April 4, 1914, with only 165 passengers aboard,

Cremating Remains
of Hasanam Koar
Feb. 2. 1914.

ਬੂੜੀ ਭਾਈ ਸਾਥ ਦੀ ... ... ਸਾਹਰ ਹੇ ਰਾਹੇ ਹੈ

111 more came aboard in Shanghai, and another 86 joined the group in Moji, Japan. There Gurdit Singh's path intersected with that of Balwant Singh, who was returning from his unsuccessful trip to India. Balwant Singh came on board to extol the passengers to rise against the British, if their entry to Canada was prevented.[6]

The ship's voyage was tracked by reporters in every port. Gurdit Singh explained their strategy in an interview: "If we are admitted we will know the Canadian government is just. If we are deported we will sue the government and if we cannot obtain redress we will go back and take up the matter with the Indian government."[7]

Balwant Singh stayed on the ship until it reached Yokohama, where an additional 14 passengers boarded. From there, the *Komagata Maru* headed across the Pacific, with 340 Sikhs, 24 Muslims and 12 Hindus on board. Twice-widowed Gurdit Singh had his seven-year-old son Balwant accompanying him on the voyage, and the passengers included two married women and four other children. The ship's imminent arrival in Vancouver stoked the fears of many about the impact of Chief Justice Hunter's decision. An editorial in the *Daily Province* on April 18 was typical:

> British Columbia has made it unmistakably clear that it will not tolerate the influx of great numbers of these Oriental coolies and that their demand for their total exclusion must be given prompt and favourable attention. To the people of this province their domestic interests are of prime importance. Imperial politics must not be allowed

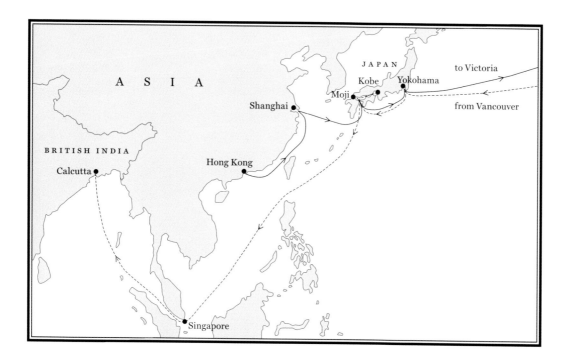

to interfere with our resolution to keep this a white country. That it should be such is for the interest of the empire to a much greater degree than satisfying the desires of an unBritish and revolutionary element in a distant part of the Empire.[8]

The same day, Vancouver MP H.H. Stevens received a letter from a friend named Pascoe Goard, who had recently returned to Canada from England. Goard was a key figure in the Christian fundamentalist movement through the British-Israel Association. In spite of its name, this anti-Semitic group saw Anglo-Saxons as "God's chosen people" and justified British colonialism.[9]

Dear H.H.

While in London I ran into a group of east Indians gathered to consider the matter of restricted emmigration [*sic*] from India to the other British territories among them this country.

An organized effort was planned to break thru the restrictions. In this country it was pointed out that the Hindoos were allowed to land as far as the detention shed and that there they could claim that they were in Canada and they could invoke the Habeas Corpus act against detention or deportation. This will be tried if they are allowed to land.

I suggest that they who are now said to coming on a Japanese boat be kept on board where they will be unable to claim such court action.

Yours truly,

Pascoe Goard[10]

LEFT This photograph was taken in Hong Kong in April 1914 on the bridge of *Komagata Maru*. Shown from left to right: Mr. Aizaki, one of the partners in the Japanese company that owned the ship; Head Engineer Kajiyama; Captain Yamamoto; and the charterer of the ship, Gurdit Singh.

ABOVE This map shows the route of the *Komagata Maru*. Many passengers who had initially signed on backed out, intimidated by the actions of British authorities in Hong Kong, but Gurdit Singh was able to attract additional passengers in the ports en route.

HINDU INVADERS NOW IN THE CITY HARBOR ON KOMAGATA MARU

Vessel Arrived Here This Morning Before Daybreak — Excited Crowd of Hindus Assemble on Waterfront — Newcomers Seem Assured of Being Admitted — Gunget Singh Issues Statement Containing Veiled Threat.

The interest that is attached to the arrival of the Japanese steamer Komagata Maru on this coast with seral hundred Hindus on board has shifted from William Head to Vancouver. The immigrant ship was granted pratique yesterday afternoon, and steamed immediately for this port. She entered Burrard Inlet some time after midnight, and anchored in the stream.

She is consigned to C. Gardner Johnson & Company, Vancouver, by her owners, Y. Sato & Company, of Kobe. She has a part cargo of Japanese coal which she will discharge here.

Mr. Malcolm J. Reid, superintendent of immigration, arrived in Vancouver from Victoria last night, the forerunner of the shifting interest in the game which opened at the William Head quarantine station and is now to be played to a conclusion in Vancouver.

As soon as the Komagata Maru had been given pratique by Dr. Nelson, the quarantine officer, the steamer started for Burrard inlet. It is understood that three immigration officers are on the steamer. A patrol launch with immigration officers on board left the boat landing stage at Pier A, a little after midnight, and did picket duty around the anchored steamer until daylight, when it was relieved by another patrol vessel. The Komagata

(Continued on Page 4.)

ABOVE Vancouver papers were filled with sensational reports and rumours days before the *Komagata Maru* finally arrived in Vancouver. The "Hindu Invasion," as it was known in the press, further fuelled the existing hysteria that had resulted from increases in Chinese and Japanese immigration (dubbed the "yellow peril").

RIGHT Soon after the ship's arrival in Vancouver, a triumphant Gurdit Singh brandishes a pair of binoculars. The man beside the lifeboat is wearing his army trench coat. The seated man wears jodhpurs and riding boots, indicating his cavalry service. To his left is one of the five women on board.

The ingenuity of Goard's suggestion was not lost on Stevens. His friend was right: Canada had not attempted to keep potential immigrants detained on ships. It was only after they had landed that "undesirable" immigrants were locked in the much-hated detention sheds, and there they always had the right of appeal. The thirty-nine Sikhs the government had sought to deport a year earlier had invoked habeas corpus, an instrument by which a prisoner could demand to be brought before a court, and not be held indefinitely or unlawfully. If the passengers of the *Komagata Maru* were allowed to land, they might try the same thing, and with the Hunter decision, there was a chance the courts would be on their side. Legally, however, onboard detention had not been tested, nor was it certain that it would be successful.

Stevens forwarded his friend's letter to W.J. Roche, federal minister for the interior, who also saw wisdom in the advice. The government now had another tool at its disposal. A new order-in-council that had come into force on March 31, four days before the *Komagata Maru*'s voyage started, barred unskilled labourers and artisans from a list of forty-two ports in British Columbia. Although never stated overtly, the regulation had clearly been passed with the *Komagata Maru* in mind. South Asians were not specified, but since most could find work in British Columbia only as artisans or unskilled labourers, the regulation targeted them.

On May 21, South Asian activists in Vancouver discovered that the recently opened harbour of Port Alberni had been excluded from the list of B.C. ports in the new regulation. The *Komagata Maru*'s radio was not working, so Husain Rahim and fellow activist Rajah Singh hired a boat and made a dash to intercept the ship before its scheduled stop in Victoria the next day.

Getting wind of the plan, Malcolm Reid, Vancouver's Dominion Immigration Agent, ordered customs agent H.L. Good to pursue them. Good bribed someone to sabotage the hired boat so that the engine would fail partway through Rahim and Singh's journey. Good's report to Reid was explicit:

> I was forced to the conclusion, that these two Hindus had every intention of diverting the vessel from her course, and were possessed of sufficient authority and power to do so. It was, therefore, my duty to prevent, by every possible means, their having communication with the vessel, thus allowing her to proceed without being spoken to, to

Victoria, thereby preventing the necessity of resorting to extreme measures, and I can assure you, sir, that they would never have had the opportunity of speaking or communicating with the vessel. Small accidents do frequently happen which disarrange the mechanism of motor boats, and on this occasion, such an accident had been provided for which I had promised the small additional sum of $25.00. The case was so important and the consequences of any interruption to the vessel's progress to William's Head Quarantine Station, were so far reaching and would have such a bad moral effect, that I considered I was justified in resorting to any means possible under the circumstances to prevent these men communicating directly or indirectly with the ship.[11]

Unaware of the small drama that had unfolded, Captain Yamamoto steered the *Komagata Maru* into Victoria's harbour, where it was scheduled to stop for health inspection. The passengers spoke to a reporter who pulled up alongside the ship in a boat. "Many of us speak English but some of us do not use the right accent. We want to talk to the pressmen." The reporter later wrote, "On board the ship were students, merchants and coolies... The majority of the men have served in the British Indian Army."[12]

167

Hopkinson and Reid saw to it no local South Asians were allowed near the ship. The accident the authorities staged to keep Husain Rahim and Rajah Singh away from the ship hinted at the strategy to come. Reid also ordered three guards placed on board for the ship's journey to Vancouver. On May 23, the ship entered Vancouver's harbour at dawn. Its 376 passengers stood on deck, dressed in their best. As hundreds watched from shore, Captain Yamamoto was ordered to drop anchor about half a mile away.

Reporters and photographers were allowed to board the ship that morning along with Vancouver immigration officials. Media representatives bombarded the man leading the "Hindu invasion." Gurdit Singh seemed confident of success, but he could not know what lay in store. Malcolm Reid declared that none of the passengers would be allowed ashore until all of them had been processed, though the ship's Japanese crew was free to come and go. All correspondence to and from the ship would be read and copied by the immigration officers who ferried it. True to his character, on May 24 Singh threatened Reid in a letter with legal action:

> I hereby notice [*sic*] you don't let me go ashore you will be held responsible for the damage which I have to suffer. You know that I'm a merchant, and there is no law to prevent the merchants to land. I have to sell my coal and have to arrange for cargo from here. I have to buy necessary provisions for the steamer. You can detain the passengers—not me.[13]

Gurdit Singh was correct in his assertion: he was not arriving as an immigrant, and there were no legal restrictions against businessmen. However, Malcolm Reid maintained to his superiors that once on shore Singh could prove to be far more troublesome, and they let the immigration agent have his way. Reid also barred the press from the ship after the first day.

The Khalsa Diwan Society and the United India League had already started to organize. A Shore Committee formed by Bhag Singh and Husain Rahim included key activists such as Sohan Lal, who acted as treasurer, and Balwant Singh. The committee displayed just the kind of unity that had disturbed Colonel Swayne, the governor of British Honduras, in 1909. They hired J. Edward Bird, who had worked the *Thirty-nine Hindus* case the year before, and whose successful defense had led to the Hunter decision—he was the only lawyer willing to represent Gurdit Singh and the passengers. Bird's attempt to get on the ship was blocked by Malcolm Reid,

TOP LEFT A veteran army signaller can be seen above the bridge on the *Komagata Maru*, using semaphore flags to send a message to shore. Another army veteran sits on the railing at bottom left, wearing his uniform. Anyone trying to signal back from shore was chased away by the police.

BOTTOM LEFT The passengers lining the railing of the *Komagata Maru* have no idea that Canada is going to set a precedent by holding them on board the ship. The ship was not allowed to dock, but instead made to anchor about half a mile from shore.

ABOVE This illustration depicting a discussion between immigration officers and Gurdit Singh appeared in *Maclean's* magazine in 1958. While largely forgotten over the years in Canada, the *Komagata Maru* story has emerged from time to time in magazines, on the radio, in theatre productions and in documentary films.

who had the support of his entire chain of command: Superintendent William Duncan Scott, Minister of the Interior W.J. Roche, Prime Minister Robert Borden and Canada's governor general, George v's uncle, the Duke of Connaught and Strathearn. Reid was also given the go-ahead to expand security on shore, hiring ex-cops and arming them with guns loaned by the local militia.

A careful assessment of Gurdit Singh's position had helped Reid to formulate a simple plan, which he communicated to Scott in a telegram. Reid realized that Singh was stretched to his financial limit, and that any delay in landing the passengers would quickly push him to the brink.

Gurdit Singh…anxious to come ashore…he has 1,500 tons of coal which he claims he must sell in order to pay his bills. There is a special clause in charter which gives right to ship agents to return ship to Hong-Kong if balance of money approximating $15,000 is not paid by June 11. Suggest he be refused permission to come ashore. He cannot raise balance money and also prevents agitation amongst local Hindoos. Can take stand that he will suffer actual bodily harm as considerable feeling existing here.[14]

Reid's superiors concurred. The *Komagata Maru* effectively became a detention shed, with Gurdit Singh and the other passengers held prisoner outside the jurisdiction of any due process. In his telegram, Reid also alluded to mob attempts to block the landing of the South Asians aboard the *Monteagle* and to the riots of 1907. The public, he intimated, would not be upset by these new violations of the rule of law.

Malcolm Reid did not trust the courts, as his letters to Scott during this time made clear: "Should these men get into the Courts, they eventually by some loophole enter Canada."[15] All the players in the drama about to unfold understood that the courts would be the ultimate battleground. For Canada, the *Komagata Maru* was a pivotal case; its outcome could have a transformative impact on immigration policy. In the worst-case scenario, the courts could build on Chief Justice Hunter's decision and throw out the continuous journey provision. There was no guarantee this would

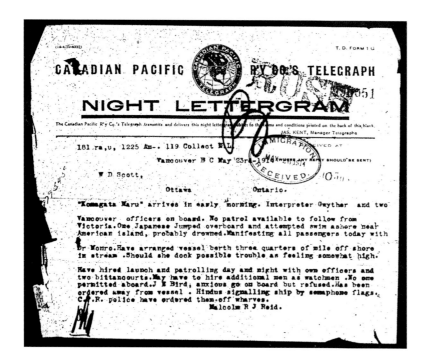

CANADIAN PACIFIC R'Y CO'S TELEGRAPH

NIGHT LETTERGRAM

The Canadian Pacific R'y Co.'s Telegraph transmits and delivers this night lettergram subject to the terms and conditions printed on the back of this blank.
JAS. KENT, Manager Telegraphs

181.ra,u, 1225 Am-. 119 Collect ML

Vancouver B C May '23rd 1914

W.D.Scott,

Ottawa   Ontario.

"Komagata Maru" arrives in early morning. Interpreter Gwyther and two

Vancouver officers on board. No patrol available to follow from
Victoria.One Japanese jumped overboard and attempted swim ashore near
American island, probably drowned.Manifesting all passengers today with

Dr Monro.Have arranged vessel berth three quarters of mile off shore
in stream .Should she dock possible trouble as feeling somewhat high.

Have hired launch and patrolling day and night with own officers and
two bittancourts.May have to hire additional men as watchmen .No one
permitted aboard.J E Bird, anxious go on board but refused.Has been
ordered away from vessel . Hindus signalling ship by semaphone flags.
C.P.R. police have ordered them off wharves.
Malcolm R J Reid.

not happen, and such a ruling could open the door for independent shipping operators like Gurdit Singh to bring in tens of thousands of South Asians. The only choice Canada would then have would be to openly discriminate against South Asians. Given the ongoing unrest in British India, imperial politics would not allow that. So the best way forward for the authorities was to block the passengers' access to the legal system. If Gurdit Singh was not able to pay the balance he owed, the ship would be recalled by its Japanese owners, rather than being turned away by Canada.

Food supplies on the ship, carefully calculated for the length of the voyage, started to run low within the first few days. Reid maintained that Gurdit Singh, not Canada, was responsible for feeding the passengers in the interim. Reid was also instructed to stretch out the first step of assessment for the ship's passengers: medical examinations. Whereas the hundreds of thousands of European immigrants arriving on Canada's east coast faced almost cursory medical examinations carried out by a small roster of overworked immigration doctors, on the *Komagata Maru* the process took not seconds, but days. Superintendent W.D. Scott had been blunt in his directive: "Get specialist, hook-worm, if necessary."[16] A common tropical affliction, the parasite was an easily treatable condition, yet was a tried and tested tactic for denying entry to South Asians. The delay was also designed to hold lawyer Edward Bird at bay.

ABOVE Immigration officers and other officials pose on one of the boats used to patrol the waters around the *Komagata Maru*. Vancouver's Stanley Park can be seen in the background of this cyanotype print. The patrols ensured that no South Asians could approach the ship from shore for direct contact with the passengers.

LEFT Former police officers drill on the wharf, armed with guns borrowed from the local militia. The *Sea Lion*, the tug used for patrols, is pictured on the left. The *Komagata Maru* appears in the background, just visible through the fog, with a smaller patrol craft in front of it.

The suave, charismatic Bird was a firm believer in the rule of law. Ignoring public anger, he took an unequivocal stand in the press on behalf of his clients: "Gurdit Singh is even more of a prisoner than if he were in a penitentiary. I have been told that if I put my foot on the gangway an immigration officer will throw me into the ocean. There is not a single thing from one cover of the immigration act to the other to authorize the authorities to take charge of that ship illegally."[17] Bird was correct in his assessment, but there was nothing he could do.

On May 28, five days after the ship's arrival, the chief legal counsel for the ministry of the interior, W.B.A. Ritchie, approached Edward Bird with a proposal: Bird would be allowed to take a test case directly to the British Columbia Court of Appeal, effectively bypassing the B.C. Supreme Court. The government's strategy was transparent. They wanted Bird to bring the habeas corpus challenge before a full panel of five judges in the Court of Appeal rather than risk the verdict of a maverick judge like Chief Justice Hunter in the B.C. Supreme Court. The majority of the five would favour the government's position, they assumed. Bird was willing to consider the offer, but the Shore Committee disagreed. They preferred to take their chances in the lower court first.

A confident Malcolm Reid had disclosed Gurdit Singh's predicament to the press, but it was a gross miscalculation. The news reports revealed an opportunity for the Shore Committee. They could raise the money owed for the charter, which would allow the ship to stay. They had eleven days to raise the $15,000. Five hundred people gathered at an urgent meeting in the Vancouver gurdwara on Second Avenue, Inspector William Hopkinson and his stenographer among them. Husain Rahim chaired the meeting. According to the stenographer's transcript, Rahim reminded the audience that the meeting had not been called to discuss larger political issues such as a mutiny. If Rahim actually did voice this disclaimer, was it because he knew Hopkinson was in the audience? Was he trying to caution his colleagues that the empire's representative was among them and they should be discreet? If a single word could evoke deep unease, or even terror, in the hearts and minds of the British, it was "mutiny." But Balwant Singh was not to be deterred. He had spent months petitioning the British in London and in India, and he used the platform of the meeting to vent his frustration in a fiery speech that invoked the Great Uprising of 1857. In British India, Hopkinson would have immediately arrested Balwant Singh for sedition, but here in Canada, even as a Dominion police officer, there was little he could do but note Balwant Singh's radical speech in his report.[18]

Such Is Life

Oriental Labor:—If you don't let me ashore I'll refuse to take anything to eat.
White Labor:—And if we do let you ashore I won't be able to get anything to eat anyway.

ABOVE Some of the strongest opposition to Asian immigration came from labour groups. Many employers used South Asian immigrants as a way to keep wages low and to undermine the fledgling union movement. The passengers on the *Komagata Maru* were seen a threat by white workers.

RIGHT The Canadian government used delay as a tactic to wear down the resolve and resources of the passengers, in the hope that the *Komagata Maru* would be recalled by its Japanese owners.

Hopkinson's account would have lethal consequences for Balwant Singh, in fact, but at the gurdwara meeting Balwant's speech pushed patriotic buttons. According to Hopkinson, Rahim urged the gathered men to donate as much as they could. One man removed his turban, turning it upside down, and placed it in front of the audience. It was a powerful symbolic gesture. The turban not only represents religious identity, it is considered the source of family pride and honour. In this instance it represented community honour. Many in attendance had come prepared, and the men lined up to throw in their money. Five thousand dollars in cash was collected, and $60,000 pledged from the future sale of real estate investments. That left a shortfall of $10,000 in hard cash. Afterwards, Hopkinson's informants told him that the money likely could not be raised. In the meantime, left with no choice, Gurdit Singh was delving into his dwindling finances to pay for provisions that were ferried to the *Komagata Maru* aboard an immigration launch.

Hopkinson and Reid were certain that the voyage of the *Komagata Maru* was part of a Ghadar Party strategy, with Gurdit Singh in on the conspiracy. Singh's statements to the press upon arrival had confirmed their fears: "What is done with this ship load of my people will determine whether we shall have peace in all parts of the British Empire. The main object of our coming here is to let the British government know how they can maintain their rule in India as the Indian government is in danger nowadays. Nationalism is growing not just in British India but in Canada as well."[19]

In the House of Commons, Frank Oliver, formerly minister of the interior and now in opposition as a Liberal MP, gave voice to Canadian nationalists: "To say that Canada shall not be able to say who shall join us in the work of building this country, that we must accept the dictation of other people as to who shall join us in that work, places us in the position not of a self governing state in a free empire, but in the position of a subordinate dependency not in control of its own affairs."[20] The same issue had emerged in 1908, when the continuous journey provision was debated, and there was still no definitive answer.

Rahim and Bird, for their parts, were writing opinion pieces in the *Hindustanee,* an English-language magazine published in Vancouver in 1913 and 1914, to present their arguments. Rahim wrote:

Sir William Osler president of the Canadian Club in England is reported to have said... "We are sorry we would if we could but you cannot come in on equal terms with Europeans. We are bound to make the country a white man's country." Such specious trash. We would if we could!... We demand equal terms with Europeans and Britishers. Nothing more, nothing less.[21]

In Bird's words,

The doctrine of a white man's country is one utterly intolerable especially for the subjects of the British Empire... If we allow *Magna Carta* to be repealed and set at naught the will of any single section of our people, there remains no reason why the British Empire should exist, since its only title to existence is that it stands for the true principles of British freedom.[22]

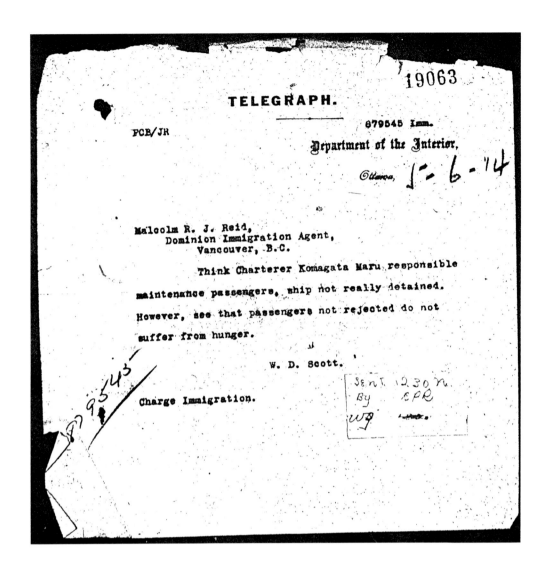

TELEGRAPH.

19063

FCB/JR

079545 Imm.

Department of the Interior,

Ottawa, 1-6-'14

Malcolm R. J. Reid,
Dominion Immigration Agent,
Vancouver, B.C.

Think Charterer Komagata Maru responsible maintenance passengers, ship not really detained. However, see that passengers not rejected do not suffer from hunger.

W. D. Scott.

Charge Immigration.

Sent 12.30 n.
By CPR
WP

Although Gurdit Singh and the Ghadarites shared a common cause, Singh had never openly supported the overthrow of colonial rule. In his memoir about the voyage, he suggests that he had been inspired by the events in South Africa, where Mohandas Gandhi had been leading a nonviolent movement for the rights of Indians. The British Empire considered the North American situation even more dangerous, because of the Punjabi majority in the community and the fact that most of those men had military connections. The Ghadar Party called not just for equal rights within the empire but for full Indian independence through an armed struggle—and it urged soldiers to mutiny. Most of the men on board the *Komagata Maru* had army contacts. They sent a plea about their predicament to the king-emperor of India, George v, but the *Kaiser-e-Hind* did not respond. Like their countrymen on shore, these passengers now felt betrayed by the Empire, and most would go on to join the Ghadar movement.

Eight days after the *Komagata Maru*'s arrival, the medical examinations were complete. Now every passenger had to appear before a board of inquiry led by Malcolm Reid. Once again the process moved at a snail's pace, with passengers being ferried one at a time to the immigration office on shore and back. On June 4, Edward Bird was finally allowed to meet with Gurdit Singh on an immigration launch positioned in between the *Komagata Maru* and the shore. They were accorded no confidentiality, as was supposed to be guaranteed by the rule of law, since immigration officers remained within earshot. Both men accepted the situation, however, since it was better than nothing. And Singh had a plan: he wanted to unload his cargo of coal and the ship's passengers, load Canadian timber onto the *Komagata Maru* and then book himself on a scheduled CP ship back to India. He offered to pay for the upkeep of the ship's passengers until they were processed and also to cover the costs if they were deported in the end.

Gurdit Singh's offer was rejected. Reid was confident in his existing strategy, and he worried that Singh, if allowed to leave, could incite trouble. Superintendent Scott agreed, but he sought to maintain the ambiguity of the situation. In a telegram to Reid, Scott reiterated that Gurdit Singh was responsible for feeding the passengers at the same time he ordered Reid to make sure that the passengers did not go hungry. More significantly, Scott stated that the passengers were "not really detained."[23] It was an astonishing admission of the government's intention to keep the passengers in legal limbo. Moreover, this internal document acknowledged their arbitrary detention, which itself was outside the law.

Over the next few days, Gurdit Singh retaliated by blocking passengers from attending the board of inquiry hearings and initiating a hunger strike among the passengers for a few days, rejecting food from even the Shore Committee. Reid was processing first the passengers he knew he could reject solely on medical grounds. At the same time, he refused to abide by Canada's Immigration Act. The law was clear: once a decision had been made to deport an immigrant, he or she could appeal to the courts. Although Section 15 of the act also stated that the "immigrant, passenger or other person shall have the right to be represented by counsel," Bird was not allowed to be present. Reid went through the motions with his board of inquiry, but he did not submit any decision, even though the law demanded that he must, thus denying Bird the opening he was waiting for.

LEFT Within the law, the *Komagata Maru*'s passengers could not be detained without cause. If they were detained, they would be able to take their case to court. For this reason, they were deliberately kept in legal limbo, with even Prime Minister Robert Borden approving of the course of action.

Among the passengers were twenty-two people who had documentation proving they had lived in Canada before the continuous journey regulation was enacted. Since they had domiciled status in Canada, there were no grounds to deport them. Reid had to let them in, and on June 9, seventeen days after their arrival, the last five of the twenty-two were taken to shore in one of the immigration patrol boats.

In Parliament, debates about immigration in general continued to rock the House. H.H. Stevens tried to get an explicit addition to the Immigration Act barring Asian immigration, but Prime Minister Borden would not touch it.[24] On June 10, Frank Oliver told his fellow MPs that in the first week of June alone, 3,500 European immigrants had arrived in Quebec. Given the economic climate, he argued, the government should make some arrangements for their well-being. Oliver then pointed to reports of several hundred Chinese men landing in Vancouver after the *Komagata Maru*'s arrival.[25] Minister Roche explained the technical reasons for their landing. Oliver accepted the explanation, but nevertheless went into a lengthy tirade about the ineffectiveness of the Chinese head tax, concluding, "The standard of

Canadian civilization is being seriously affected by the large and increasing numbers of Chinese who are coming into Canada."[26]

The same day, Husain Rahim appeared at the Japanese shipping company's Vancouver office, carrying $11,000 and requesting more time to bring in the remaining $4,000. Ten days later, he delivered. The Shore Committee had pulled it off, raising nearly $18,000. Husain Rahim and Bhag Singh, not Gurdit Singh, were now in control of the ship. But while Reid's plan had now evaporated, pressure was building on the Shore Committee. The additional $3,000 available to provision the ship would not last long, and the government still held the cards in its ability to delay. Now that he was officially the charterer, Rahim demanded access to the cargo of coal on the ship to gain more money for food and supplies for the passengers. Predictably, Reid refused. Realizing they could not extend the standoff indefinitely, Bhag Singh and Husain Rahim directed Edward Bird to seek a deal with the government. The Shore Committee did not consult on this with Gurdit Singh, presumably since there was no way to have a confidential discussion with him.

On June 12, Parliament adjourned for the summer. H.H. Stevens returned to Vancouver, and Minister Roche went on vacation. Eight days later, as the Shore Committee waited for the government to respond, two Japanese warships sailed into Vancouver. Fifty years later, in a radio interview, H.H. Stevens expressed strong feelings about what he still considered a missed opportunity with respect to the *Komagata Maru*'s passengers. "They should have been returned on any ship that could be induced to take them, and it could have been, in my opinion, a wise thing to have turned this *Komagata Maru* crew over to the Japanese cruisers, because the ship belonged to Japan and the cruisers could have taken whatever steps necessary to put their own captain and Japanese crew in charge of their own ship."[27] But the Imperial Japanese Navy refused to be drawn into what was clearly an internal matter for Canada.

It Looks Like This

The doorkeeper:—If I let you get your foot inside, will you promise to stay out.

ABOVE Not everyone was certain that Prime Minister Robert Borden would be able to stop the South Asian immigrants from landing. There was tremendous anxiety that lawyer Edward Bird would successfully defend their case in court.

UNDESIRABLES

Both sides worked to mobilize public opinion. The Shore Committee held a public meeting in downtown Vancouver, with Rahim chairing. Hopkinson attended, as usual, as did about 125 members of the Socialist Party and four hundred South Asians.[28] Bird outlined in detail for the assembled the legal situation as he saw it. He wanted the government to know he and others saw through their strategy: "I can only surmise that the instructions from the Department at Ottawa to the Immigration authorities here was to delay matters and delay matters and procrastinate and delay until such a time as these people were starved back to their original port from whence they sailed." Bird refused to be intimidated or silenced by Hopkinson's presence. "The immigration department is the most autocratic of our institutions and is managed by law-defying anarchists who have told me they do not know if they will abide by the Supreme Court orders if they let the passengers stay in Canada."[29]

There was growing fear and resentment that Edward Bird might win in court yet again. A letter to the editor appearing in the *Daily Province* summed up the mood: "The government passes a law and they seem to tremble in their boots for fear that Mr. Bird will say it is unconstitutional and the majority of people are in the same state."

On June 23, H.H. Stevens and T.S. Baxter, the mayor of Vancouver, called their own meeting. Two thousand people attended. Stevens, a seasoned politician and public speaker, cut to the core of the issue and offered a rebuttal:

> What we face in British Columbia and in Canada today is this—whether or not the civilization which finds its highest exemplification in the Anglo-Saxon British rule shall or shall not prevail in the dominion of Canada. We have on the bench of British Columbia today, men who are willing to give a decision contrary to the general public opinion and contrary to what is the clear meaning of the Immigration Act. Some people say, why don't you go to the courts with your case? We are prepared to go to the courts if we can get a fair court to go to.[30]

The June 23 meeting passed a unanimous resolution urging the federal government to deport the passengers on the *Komagata Maru*. But Stevens's attack on the judiciary did not go unnoticed by the press, who felt he had gone too far. Ignoring the rule of law was one thing, but casting aspersions on the courts was another.

As before, government lawyers offered Edward Bird a single test case that would go directly to the B.C. Court of Appeal. Bird agreed, but he was still not allowed to board the ship. This time he appealed directly by telegram to the prime minister, a fellow lawyer, to obtain access to his clients: "Immigration inspector says he has wire from Minister refusing me right to board ship. Please withdraw these instructions and allow me full privileges of counsel."[31] Aware that Bird was planning to complain to Ottawa, Malcolm Reid had already wired his boss, Superintendent Scott, in his typical staccato fashion: "Bird wiring to get your consent to go on board *Komagata Maru* ... Advisable not permit him have arranged give interview clients from another launch if desired."[32] Scott agreed with this suggested degree of access, as did the deputy minister of the interior. Borden's response to Bird was concise: "Immigration officials inform me suitable arrangements were communicated to you for the purpose of seeing clients."[33]

Everyone from Reid and on up chose to deny Bird the "full privileges of counsel" that the law of the land guaranteed. Instead, two men were ferried ashore after Bird selected their names from the passenger list. Bird spent a couple of hours interviewing them, then chose Munshi Singh, a twenty-six-year-old farmer. It was only now that the board of inquiry led by Reid issued a decision: Munshi Singh was ordered to be deported. Bird applied to the B.C. Supreme Court for a writ of habeas corpus to contest the legality of his client's detention. The case was dismissed by the Supreme Court so that it could move to the Court of Appeal. Munshi Singh was detained on shore and taken to Victoria four days later for the trial. Public anxiety about the pending case was articulated by a Vancouver newspaper, the *Sunset:*

> The sister dominion declared for a "White Australia," and that policy is being enforced to the letter. How will Canada choose? Will it be a weak-kneed policy of "a few Japanese, as many Chinese as can pay the head tax and a limited number of Hindus" or a "White Canada"?[34]

Edward Bird presented his arguments to the five appeals-court judges. Using Munshi Singh as an example, he argued that, like Canadians, the passengers on the *Komagata Maru* were British subjects; they could not be considered aliens. Bird stressed that Canada could not legally discriminate against British subjects along racial lines. Finally, he reached for the bedrock of British common law, the Magna Carta, to argue that Munshi Singh was being denied his civil rights.

As Shore Committee leaders watched the courtroom drama unfold, Malcolm Reid maintained pressure on the ship. He used his own discretion to determine when food and water would be delivered to the passengers, at times pushing them to the edge of unbearable thirst and starvation. The Japanese crew was still allowed free access to shore, but a strict embargo enforced by Reid ensured that no drinking water reached the passengers. They sent out a desperate plea, to no avail. "There is no supply of water since forty-eight hours. And there is not a single drop of water to drink. If water is not supplied within an hour, a few passengers will breathe their last, and the result will be very bad."[35]

Hopkinson hoped the passengers would take out their anger on Gurdit Singh, and he had said as much in his report to his superior in the Department of Criminal Intelligence in British India, J.A. Wallinger: "It is possible that Gurdit Singh, will receive rough treatment at the hands of those on board if no provisions are forthcoming."[36] But that wasn't what happened. Singh later recalled in his memoir the desperation of the passengers when the Japanese crew brought on board their barrel of water as usual: "The passengers being mad with thirst, lost all control... Oh, it was an awful sight to see... Some tried to take water in their cups, some licked the spilled water and others moistened their lips by soaking cloth... Religious and caste prejudices were forgotten... Everybody considered his own life more precious than the other and was anxious to save it."[37] And the passengers not only seized the water, they took over the ship.

In Victoria, government lawyers argued that Munshi Singh had not come to Canada by continuous journey from India, he did not have $200 in his possession and he was an unskilled labourer. Pointing out the limited rights extended to "native Indians," the lawyers argued that Canada did have the power to restrict the rights of British subjects by reason of their race.[38] In effect, the colonization of Canada and the subjugation of its aboriginal inhabitants was presented as a legitimate precedent for denying South Asians their rights. The court adjourned for a week to allow the judges to deliberate.

On July 6, the judges of the Court of Appeal reconvened to present their unanimous decision: Munshi Singh could not be admitted to Canada, for a variety of reasons. The continuous journey regulation had been violated, since the *Komagata Maru* had originated in Hong Kong, not India. Munshi Singh would be an unskilled labourer in Canada, and hence was barred under that recently passed regulation. The court also asserted that, as a self-governing dominion of the British Empire, Canada had the right to determine who got in and was also within its constitutional rights to bar British subjects. One of the learned judges went even further, offering

BELOW This photo may depict
lawyer J. Edward Bird leaving the
Komagata Maru. Bird was denied
access to the passengers he was
hired to defend, and allowed on
board only once the court had ruled
against them.

some advice to the unequal British subjects: "Better that peoples of non-assimilative—and by nature properly non-assimilative—race should not come to Canada, but rather, that they should remain of residence in their country of origin and there do their share, as they have in the past, in the preservation and development of the Empire."[39]

Canada now had complete control over its gates. The Montreal *Gazette* expressed ambivalence: "It was not an act of Christian policy to shut them out. It may yet be found it was not an act of statesmanship."[40] But the *Times* of London had no qualms: "The judgment finally disposes of the idea that British citizenship in itself confers an unrestricted right of entrance into any part of the British Dominions."[41]

An immigration boat took Edward Bird out to the *Komagata Maru*. He shouted the news about the decisive loss to the passengers, who though still combative had returned control of the ship to Captain Yamamoto. The next day, Bird was finally allowed to board the ship and to meet with Gurdit Singh in private for the first time. An appeal to the Supreme Court of Canada was impossible, both men knew; the court was closed for the summer and would not reconvene until the fall. A direct appeal to the Privy Council in London, the highest court in the British Empire, would take longer. Gurdit wanted to unload the cargo of coal and load Canadian timber to make up for his losses, but the government had refused. It remained to be seen who would provision the ship for the return voyage.

The ship's passengers had been living day to day on the supplies sent to them by the Shore Committee, and immigration officials expected that to continue. Bird sent a terse letter to Inspector Reid on the committee's behalf: "I have seen Mr. Rahim, one of the charterers, this morning and he says he does not propose to send any more food or water to the Ship. He puts the whole burden upon the Government." Bird copied this letter to Malcolm Reid and added: "I would urge most strongly upon you that these men be not allowed to suffer further."[42]

JUDGES FIND UNANIMOUSLY AGAINST MUNCHI SINGH IN HABEAS CORPUS APPEAL

Immigration Board Upheld on All Points—Orders-in-Council Declared Valid by Judges.

JAPANESE CONSUL ASSERTS HIS AUTHORITY

State of Anarchy Aboard Komagata Not to be Allowed to Continue.

VICTORIA, B. C., July 6.—Court unanimously dismissed Hindoo appeal upholding immigration authorities at every point.

Efforts of the Hindoos aboard the Komagata Maru to break through the immigration regulations were defeated this morning, when the court of appeals handed down a decision in the case of Munchi Singh and Malcolm Reid, for whom a writ of habeas corpus was asked by Mr. J. Edward Bird.

GURDIT SINGH
Leader of the Hindoo Party Aboard the Komagata.

ABOVE Munshi Singh was ordered deported on July 6, 1914. The B.C. Court of Appeal ruled that he could not land in Canada because he did not meet the conditions set out in the orders-in-council. The court also ruled that Canada could discriminate against fellow British subjects.

But the ship's continuing presence in the harbour after the court decision was causing the public mood in Vancouver to turn nasty, and Bird himself was under increasing attack. As he would reveal in a later memoir: "I remember getting... a letter from some busy-body who wrote and threatened that I would be shot if I did not drop the case... I found it was not considered by others as a joke as my wife was phoned to urge me to leave town for a time."[43] His life insurance company had even cancelled his policy. Bird had fought for the maintenance of the rule of law in Canada and for the equality and dignity of all. There was nothing more he could do. Concerned for the safety of his wife and two young sons, he agreed to take a short vacation. His partners took over the task of final negotiations with the government.

Water continued to be in short supply on the ship. The passengers wrote to Reid, "Take pity on our wretched condition, otherwise we shall be compelled to get ashore to quench our raging thirst." Their plea fell on deaf ears.[44]

When the ship was still in the harbour ten days after the verdict had come down, Borden demanded an explanation. Immigration officials informed the prime minister that Gurdit Singh had refused their offer, agreed to by the ship's owners, that the *Komagata Maru* would be provisioned only after it reached the boundary with international waters. Reid was allowing only minimal supplies of food and water to be delivered, and the children in particular were suffering. As Gurdit Singh wrote in his later account: "One day a child... named Fouja Singh... fainted due to thirst. His mother began to weep. It was a heart-rending scene. I hastened to the cabin of the captain... and brought a bottle of beer. As soon as a few spoons of it were put into his mouth, the child began to regain his senses. But the Japanese felt very much offended at my bringing the bottle of beer from their Captain's cabin."[45] Passengers once again seized the ship from the Japanese crew, mistrustful that food would be delivered once the ship was outside of Canadian waters.

H.H. Stevens urged Mayor Baxter to act. The mayor planned to mobilize the police force to help the Japanese crew regain control of the *Komagata Maru*, but William Hopkinson was anxious about this tactic; he knew any use of force on Canadian soil would have dire consequences in India. His report to J.A. Wallinger was carefully worded: "I had come there with the object, if possible, of avoiding any conflict between the officers of the law and the passengers of the boat... I was informed that neither the ship nor the passengers on the boat would leave the harbour unless they received in writing permission from Bhag Singh and Rahim... I informed [them] that unfortunately Bhag Singh had been arrested by the United

The *Komagata Maru* at the Gates of Canada   *121*

States, along with him was Balwant Singh ... Rahim ... in all probability was in the hands of the law."[46]

Bhag Singh and Balwant Singh had ventured across the border to meet with the leaders of the Ghadar Party, and Hopkinson had used his U.S. contacts to make sure that both men were detained by American immigration officers. Each had a revolver and bullets with him; not exactly a crime in the United States, but a good enough ruse for authorities to use in ensuring that the troublesome activists were removed from the scene. The charges of carrying weapons would be dropped a week later, but for the moment Hopkinson had crippled the Shore Committee. And he had lied to Gurdit Singh and the passengers about Husain Rahim, who was still in Vancouver.

Just past midnight on July 19, the *Sea Lion*, the largest tug in the city, was called into action. Interviewed for a CBC radio documentary in 1964, H.H. Stevens described the chain of events: "So the Immigration authorities, Mr. Reid and Hopkinson and myself along with a hundred and fifty policemen who were asked to assist, were aboard the *Sea Lion* and set out to abort the *Komagata Maru* in order to place back the ship in the control of its Captain. As we approached the ship, those aboard, the Hindus aboard, were antagonistic, and there was a good deal of shouting."[47]

If Stevens had anticipated that the ship's passengers would accept their assigned role as legally defeated, hence subjugated, people, he was mistaken. The police seemed to have forgotten that many of those on board were battle-hardened veterans, trained to fight to the last man. As the *Sea Lion* came within a stone's throw of the *Komagata Maru,* pieces of coal and other improvised projectiles rained down from the much higher deck of the ship. Several windows on the tugboat were smashed, and many policemen were injured.

The *Sea Lion* turned back, and Hopkinson's subsequent report cleverly hinted at the bogey of an armed mutiny: "[It] is believed that three revolver shots were fired from the Japanese boat by the Hindus. Fortunately, none of them took effect."[48] Stevens, in his urgent telegram to the prime minister, made no mention of this supposed armed escalation:

> Hindus on ship apparently desperately revolutionary and determined to defy Law. Absolutely necessary that some strong stance be taken and would urge that Rainbow or some naval department vessel be detailed to take charge of the situation.[49]

No other account of these events mentions the alleged shooting, but it became part of the official government record that "several shots were fired."[50] By then, Borden had had enough. As Stevens had proposed, the prime minister called in the HMCS *Rainbow,* one half of the newly formed Royal Canadian Navy. This second-hand cruiser had served with the British Royal Navy, and the *Rainbow* had seen action in Canada once before—it had been used to quell a workers' strike in Prince Rupert, British Columbia. Now it was about to be used against fellow subjects of the British Empire.

William Hopkinson's reports about the turning back of the *Sea Lion* were met with alarm in Britain and India. Lord Hardinge, the viceroy of India, warned London, and the colonial secretary in turn wired Borden immediately: "Very advisable to avoid use of force which would have extremely bad effect in Punjab."[51] The

LEFT The three key players on the government side speak with reporters. William Hopkinson, the British intelligence officer and Canadian immigration inspector, is on the far right, with Dominion Immigration Agent Malcolm Reid (in uniform) and MP H.H. Stevens in the middle.

RIGHT The HMCS *Rainbow*, one half of the fledgling Royal Canadian Navy, is shown in the foreground, with the *Komagata Maru* behind. The second-hand British warship had already been used to quell a strike in Prince Rupert, B.C.

BELOW Once the Canadian government agreed to provision the *Komagata Maru,* the defiant passengers gave control back to the Japanese crew. According to reports, the passengers joked and inquired about the injuries suffered by the policemen who had attacked them.

prime minister wired Martin Burrell, his minister of agriculture, who was vaca-
tioning in British Columbia, on his farm in Penticton, in Burrell's home riding of
Yale-Cariboo: "Think it highly desirable that you proceed immediately to Vancouver
and report on situation."[52] Burrell was the only cabinet minister from British
Columbia. Immigration was certainly not in his portfolio, though he had a wide
breadth of experience. Burrell had emigrated to Canada from England as a young
man; he had worked as a bank clerk, a fruit farmer and a lecturer, and he now owned
the largest apple tree nursery in British Columbia. As a Brit, Burrell was aware of
the geopolitics of the empire, and he was a known supporter of South Asian exclusion. The prime minister wanted a perspective on the events that he could fully trust.
The reports from Vancouver to date had been driven by the personal agendas of Reid,
Hopkinson and Stevens.

By the time Martin Burrell arrived in Vancouver, the city was in a state of high
excitement. Thousands of people lined the waterfront watching the drama unfold
on the water and on land. Dozens of small watercraft were in the harbour near the
Komagata Maru and the *Rainbow*. A few days earlier the federal government had
put the three regiments of the Canadian militia stationed in Vancouver on standby.
Citing fears of rioting, the chief of police urged the mayor to deploy the troops.[53] On
July 20, fully armed soldiers of the Duke of Connaught's Sixth Regiment, the Irish
Fusiliers and the Scottish Highlanders marched through the city to the waterfront,
ready to board the *Rainbow*.[54]

The passengers on the *Komagata Maru* were not intimidated by this show of
force. As Gurdit Singh later wrote: "It was agreed that it was an impossibility to
fight and win against such fearful odds… The warship was preparing for action and
on the other hand we were preparing for death. On behalf of the Government the
commander sent the message. 'Leave our shores, you uninvited Indians, or we fire.'
Our reply to this command was that if Canada will allow us to provision the ship we
will go, otherwise, 'Fire away. We prefer death here than on the high seas.'"[55]

Robert Borden, sure of a conspiracy, wrote to the governor general: "We are more
and more convinced that the attempt to have these Hindus enter Canada is but one
instance of a deliberate plot to foment sedition."[56]

Martin Burrell understood that he had to defuse the situation. Commander
Walter Hose, captain of the *Rainbow*, had advised him that if militiamen were
to storm the ship, at least a hundred lives could be lost.[57] Moving quickly, Burrell
sought a direct meeting with Husain Rahim and offered to pay for the provisions for

ABOVE Martin Burrell, the federal
minister of agriculture asked by
Borden to resolve the *Komagata
Maru* crisis, had told the Canadian
Club in 1912: "The question of Hindu
women's immigration … is the domi-
nant question of the whole empire.
It is a question of the … final supremacy of the yellow or the white."

RIGHT The Canadian militia was mobilized to take over the ship by force. Soldiers of the Irish Fusiliers, the Sixth Regiment (Duke of Connaught's Own Rifles) and the Seaforth Highlanders assemble at the pier, ready to spring into action if necessary. In the far background lies their target, the *Komagata Maru*.

BELOW Inspector Reid, H.H. Stevens and Commander Hose of the HMCS *Rainbow* confer with a militia officer. Canadian officers had anticipated the loss of dozens of lives if they were ordered to seize the *Komagata Maru* by force, but Minister Burrell arranged instead to provision the ship for its return journey.

285

the return voyage. Rahim countered with another demand: the Shore Committee had incurred the expenses of the charter and feeding the passengers, and Rahim wanted them to be reimbursed for the $25,000 they had spent.

Invoking the notion of British fair play and justice, Martin Burrell countered by offering the Shore Committee an inquiry once the ship had left Canada: "As a member of the Government I shall wire to the PM, ask that the claims are thoroughly examined by an imperial commissioner and will urge that full and sympathetic consideration be given to all those who deserve generous treatment."[58] Burrell had chosen his words carefully, as he would later reassure Borden in a confidential memo: "You will notice I have not given any definite pledge of meeting these claims."[59]

ABOVE Members of the Shore Committee were finally allowed aboard to meet the *Komagata Maru*'s passengers on July 22, 1914. The committee sought to recoup the $25,000 they had spent on the charter of the ship and on provisions, but a federally appointed imperial commissioner denied their claim.

Will the Dyke Hold?

Or will certain interests, under the guise of imperial needs, flood our country with cheap and unskilled labor?

LEFT This editorial cartoon, prompted by the *Komagata Maru's* presence, graphically illustrates core Canadian anxieties. Once the Canadian "dyke" (the country's racist immigration laws) had been upheld by the B.C. Court of Appeal, Canada was willing to use military force to turn away the ship.

BELOW Thousands of Vancouverites gathered on shore to watch the departure of the *Komagata Maru*, shown in the far background with the *Rainbow* in front. Dozens of small pleasure craft carrying sightseers and picnickers surrounded the ship once it was announced it would finally be turned away.

The committee would never get their money back, as it turned out. But they took the bait Burrell held out, and while provisions were being gathered the minister gave the Shore Committee permission to go on board the *Komagata Maru*. As committee members headed out to the ship, Malcolm Reid instructed the commander of the militia to line up his men on shore: "I asked Col. Duff-Stewart to parade his men with fixed bayonets, and 200 men were drawn up and the local committee passed thru the ranks. This I think had a good moral effect, as there had been considerable doubt expressed by the Hindus as to any drastic action being ever taken."[60]

After two months, Husain Rahim and other Shore Committee members finally met the passengers they had tried so hard to defend and to land. The defiant mood on board the ship surprised them, as Vancouver resident G.S. Bilga later recounted in an interview:

> Their point [was] this: "If we do go back, where I am going to? What are we going to do? We have nothing left. If we go back to India, we know the Indian government will not give us any assistance at all. They might arrest us and put us in jail. So why not we die here, instead of going back to die there?" We explained to them that we are not happy that you are going back, but our hands are tied. We don't have any resources, we don't have any power, to fight with. So the best way is for you people to go back."[61]

On July 23, the *Komagata Maru* finally lifted its anchor. Escorted by the HMCS *Rainbow*, it headed out to the Pacific.

BELOW The turning away of the *Komagata Maru* would soon be overshadowed by the outbreak of the First World War. By the time the passengers arrived in British India in October, imperial authorities had deemed them to be subversive and seditious. A confrontation ensued once they finally landed; British troops opened fire and twenty-one people were killed.

The *Komagata Maru* at the Gates of Canada

EPILOGUE

BRITAIN, AND BY extension the British Empire, declared war on Germany on
August 4, 1914, and Canada soon forgot about the *Komagata Maru*. More than
1.3 million Indian soldiers and labourers volunteered to fight for Britain in Europe
and the Middle East. During the early stages of the war, it was the British Indian
Army who helped hold the Germans at bay on Europe's Western Front. At least a
dozen South Asians, mainly Sikhs, joined the Canadian Expeditionary Force.[1]

In Vancouver, the South Asian community imploded. Two men identified as
agents for Inspector William Hopkinson were found murdered. And in September
Hopkinson's main agent, Bela Singh, was cornered in the Sikh temple. Before
dozens of witnesses, he shot his way out, injuring nine and killing two. One of the
dead was Bhag Singh, a leader of the Shore Committee and one of the temple's
granthis.

The Ghadar Party used the turning away of the *Komagata Maru* to encourage
South Asian men to leave North America and join the planned uprising in India.
Thousands of copies of *Ghadar* magazine were circulated. The call that went out
was simple: "Wanted—8000 Ghadarites. Pay—death. Reward—Freedom." A book
of poetry called *Ghadar di Goonj*—Echoes of Mutiny—was published to reinforce
patriotic resolve.

RIGHT This propaganda postcard from 1914 extols the unity of troops from Great Britain, Canada, Australia and British India. The latter's 1.3 million soldiers formed the largest volunteer army to fight in the war.

BELOW This postcard says it all. However, while Canada and the white dominions of Australia and New Zealand emerged as more sovereign and mature nations after the war, British India did not. In spite of the sacrifice of more than 74,000 troops, the country was denied Dominion status.

BELOW This German postcard
shows the soldiers of the Indian
Corps attacking German trenches
during the First Battle of Ypres.
German artists and photographers
were fascinated by the South Asian
troops. South Asian prisoners of war
were encouraged to switch sides and
convince their compatriots to desert,
but to no avail.

RIGHT The Indian Corps in Marseilles, France, in September 1914. A month later, they were in the First Battle of Ypres. The corps prevented a strategically disastrous German breakthrough to the sea, yet most accounts of the First World War don't mention their significant role.

BELOW A rare postcard showing British Indian Army soldiers with Canadian, Australian and French troops in France in 1917. At least a dozen South Asian Canadians, both Sikhs and Muslims, also served in the Canadian Expeditionary Force.

CAMPAGNE. 1914 - Armée des Indes
Arrivée d'un détachement Hindous
à Marseille - L.R.

" Le 14 Juillet à PARIS en 1916 " — Nos Alliés

We are the children of the Nation
The Nation is our father
We will throw out the British
We will rule ourselves
There is no politics that we don't know
There is no business that we don't know
Hindu rule you just push aside
Muslim rule you brush aside
And others fear the Sikh rule
After the British we will rule[2]

Thousands returned to India to wage war against the king-emperor. However, thanks mainly to Hopkinson's continued reports, the empire was on high alert. In 1914 British India had passed the Ingress into India Ordinance, which gave it sweeping powers to detain all South Asians returning from North America. Hundreds were arrested. Sensing that the ship's passengers would be ripe for recruitment, Ghadar party leaders had arranged to meet the *Komagata Maru* in Japan during its return voyage. They exploited the deep betrayal the passengers felt and reminded them once again that South Asians would not be treated as equals as long as their country remained under British rule.

On September 26, two months after sailing out from Vancouver's harbour, the *Komagata Maru* reached the coast of British India. Imperial authorities, convinced that the passengers were Ghadarites, or at the very least seditious, apprehended the ship offshore. They combed it for weapons over the next three days but found nothing.

The ship was then diverted to the town of Budge Budge, 17 miles short of its final destination, Calcutta. The journey had been arduous, and by now the passengers had been on board the ship for more than four months. They saw the diversion as another trick, and tensions ran high. Authorities wanted the passengers to take a special train to the Punjab, but most did not trust the police force that had been sent to greet them. Only a few agreed to get on the train, and the others, led by Gurdit Singh, decided to make their way to Calcutta on foot. When police blocked the procession,

ABOVE These cavalrymen of the Deccan Horse, a British Indian Army regiment, served as infantry troops in the trenches on the Western Front in France. The Indian Corps outnumbered the British Expeditionary Force in Europe, and over nine thousand soldiers of the corps lie buried in France.

ABOVE This print by British artist R. Woodruff is entitled *For the Glory of the Raj: Indian Troops Charging the German Trenches at Neuve Chapelle.* Over 4,700 South Asian men died in this almost forgotten battle in March 1915. British Indian cavalrymen and Canadian troops fought together again at Passchendaele in 1917.

a scuffle broke out, and Gurdit Singh's son was snatched away from him. He later wrote: "I understood at once the meaning of this act ... and to our horror we felt the police bullets hitting us. No warning of whatever nature was given for this unprovoked attack ... Three or four of my men lifted me on their shoulders and carried me to safety. I protested ... but they replied, 'Alive, you will tell the world the sad story of the *Komagata Maru.*'"[3] Singh and a few other passengers escaped, but the rest of the passengers were rounded up and arrested. Twenty-two people were killed, including a British official, and nearly two dozen passengers suffered bullet wounds.[4]

Revolutionaries in the Punjab considered what happened at Budge Budge a massacre, but prominent Indian nationalist leaders believed the government's story that the passengers had started a riot. Gurdit Singh went underground, and Ghadar revolutionaries thought he had been killed.

In October, during a debate about Asian immigration in the House of Commons, Wilfrid Laurier, now leader of the Opposition, alluded to the turning away of the *Komagata Maru:* "The people of Canada want to have a white country, and certain

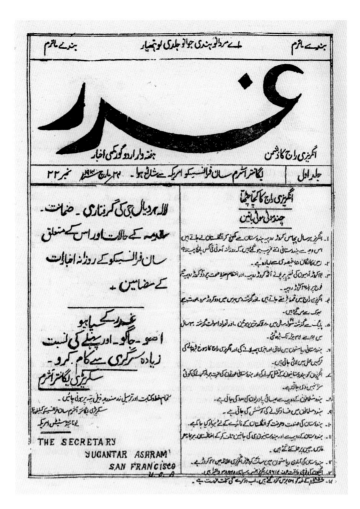

LEFT The Ghadar (Mutiny) Party drew its name from the title of its newspaper, printed in both Urdu and Punjabi. The turning away of the *Komagata Maru* was used to issue a patriotic call for South Asians to return to British India and take up arms against the British. Thousands went back.

BELOW Violence erupted within the community as intelligence agents were exposed, and four people were killed. The fifth victim was British intelligence agent William Hopkinson. His assassin Mewa Singh gave himself up after the shooting. Hopkinson's funeral drew the largest gathering of law enforcement officers from Canada and the United States that Vancouver had seen.

ABOVE William Hopkinson's body was carried in a Union Jack–draped coffin. Hopkinson's intelligence network was maintained after his death, and South Asian activists were kept under surveillance during the First World War.

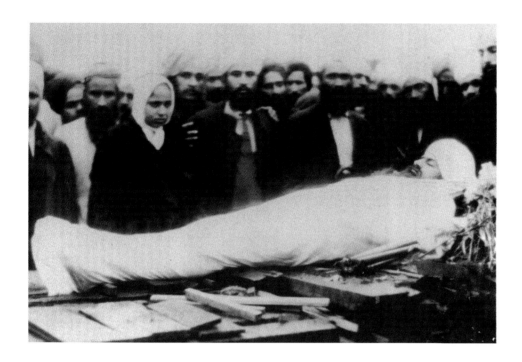

LEFT William Hopkinson's assassin, Mewa Singh, was hanged in January 1915. This photo shows his body lying on a funeral pyre just before his cremation in Vancouver. Singh was hailed as a martyr, and his portrait still appears in some of the older Sikh temples in British Columbia.

BELOW Forty-seven mutineers from the Fifth Light Infantry were executed by firing squad in Singapore in 1915. The British Indian Army unit, composed of Hindustani Muslim soldiers, had mutinied over rumours that they were being sent to Mesopotamia to fight against Turkish forces. They were thought to have been influenced by Ghadar propaganda.

Kartar Singh   Gurdit Singh   Kanshi Ram   Amir Chand   Rahmat Ali Shah

Sohan Lal   V.G. Pingle   Jiwan Singh   Jagat Singh   Kehar Singh

ABOVE After evading arrest, Gurdit Singh went underground for years. A Ghadar Party publication from 1917 wrongly presumed Gurdit Singh was hanged when it published these portraits with the caption "India's Martyrs: The above are among the 400 who have been hanged during 1915 and 1916." However Sohan Lal and Harnam Singh, both members of the Vancouver Shore Committee, were arrested, tried and hanged.

of our fellow subjects who are not of the white race want to come to Canada and be admitted to all the rights of Canadian citizenship . . . These men have been taught by a certain school of politics that they are equals of British subjects; unfortunately they are brought face to face with the hard facts when it's too late."[5]

Bela Singh's trial began at the Vancouver courthouse on October 21. As William Hopkinson waited outside the courtroom to testify on his agent's behalf, he was approached by a quiet and devout Sikh named Mewa Singh. Without warning, Mewa Singh shot Hopkinson dead and then gave himself up to police. Bela Singh, despite having killed two people, was acquitted, but Mewa Singh was swiftly brought to trial. He defended his actions in a long speech saying, "If the police and administration join together in perpetrating injustice, somebody must rise against it. You may hang me. What more can you do?"[6] Hanged on January 11, 1915, Mewa Singh became an icon of the Ghadar revolution.

In February 1915, the Ghadar Party managed to incite a British Indian Army regiment stationed in Singapore to mutiny. The battle lasted less than a week, ending with forty-seven mutineers being publicly executed by firing squad. In British India, the Ghadar movement was brutally crushed. Between 1915 and 1917, the Lahore Conspiracy trials were held in Punjab. Special tribunals heard secret evidence, denied the accused access to lawyers and offered no right of appeal.

Forty-two men were sentenced to death for "conspiring to wage war against the King Emperor," including Balwant Singh, the Vancouver Sikh temple's *granthi*.[7] The main evidence against him was Hopkinson's notes about the speech Balwant Singh had given at the meeting held to raise funds for the *Komagata Maru*. Also hanged was the treasurer of the Shore Committee, Sohan Lal. Fearing a similar fate if he returned to British India, Husain Rahim stayed on in Canada.

In November 1921, after years in hiding, Gurdit Singh met Mohandas Gandhi, who had emerged as the leader of the nationalist movement. According to Singh's memoir, Gandhi told him "it was not much creditable [*sic*] for him to roam hither and thither disguising himself—he who once shook the Government and made a voyage to Canada, awoke the sleeping India and exposed the bureaucratic policy

Sikh Temple - Victoria, B.C. November 5, 1939.
Final visit of Dr. D. P. PANDIA
before departure from Canada.

before…he whose adventures helped the Indians in Africa in their distressed condition; I think his demise for country's sake will bring forth some good for the country."[8] But the British could not afford to make a martyr of Gurdit Singh. He was not hanged, though he was imprisoned for five years. Sixty-eight years old when he was released, Singh tried to keep the memory of the *Komagata Maru* alive and mounted an unsuccessful attempt to recover his business assets.

By 1941, there were only about 1,400 South Asians living in Canada. Dr. Pandia, who had served Gandhi's personal secretary for a time, moved to Vancouver and became the community's main advocate for equal rights. On January 1, 1947, the Canadian Citizenship Act came into force, and three months later, on April 2, South Asians became full citizens of Canada and regained the right to vote. The continuous journey regulation was removed from the Immigration Act the next year—ironically, by a government led by Prime Minister Mackenzie King, who as a young man had written the regulation. Yet race- and nationality-based criteria remained part of Canada's immigration policy. Under the Immigration Act of 1952, immigrants could be refused admission for reasons including nationality, ethnicity, geographic area of origin and "unsuitability" with regard to the climate. At the same time a quota system was adopted—one that limited immigrants from the newly independent nations of South Asia. Annually, Canada would allow 150 immigrants from India, 100 from Pakistan and 50 from Ceylon. In 1962 the quotas were abolished, but "assimability" remained part of the criteria until 1967, when a points-based assessment system was introduced.

On August 15, 1947, amidst the genocide of more than fifteen million people, British India was partitioned into India and Pakistan. With that died the Ghadar dream of a United States of India. However, some of the Ghadar ideas survived. On January 26, 1950, India emerged with a brand-new constitution describing it as a secular socialist republic.

Gurdit Singh died on July 24, 1953—almost thirty-nine years to the day from the date the *Komagata Maru* became the first ship bearing migrants to be turned away from Canadian shores. Half a century later, in 2006, Gurdit Singh's great-grandson, Tejpal Singh Sandhu, arrived in Canada with his wife and infant son.

LEFT Dr. D.P. Pandia (the clean-shaven man shown front row centre), a lawyer, was instrumental in helping the South Asian community in Canada get back the right to vote in 1948. That same year, the continuous journey regulation was removed from the Immigration Act.

NOTES

INTRODUCTION

1. W.L.M. King, "Report by W. L. Mackenzie King, C.M.G., Deputy Minister of Labour, on Mission to England to Confer with British Authorities of the Subject of Immigration to Canada from the Orient and Immigration from India in Particular," *Sessional Papers 1908*, no. 36a, Library and Archives Canada.

2. G.S. Basran and B. Singh Bolaria, *The Sikhs in Canada: Migration, Race, Class and Gender* (New York: Oxford University Press, 2003).

3. Patwant Singh, *The Sikhs* (New York: Knopf, 2000), p. 233.

4. People's Union for Democratic Rights and People's Union for Civil Liberties, *Who Are the Guilty? Report of a Joint Inquiry into the Causes and Impact of the Riots in Delhi from 31 October to 10 November, 1984* (New Delhi: PUDR & PUCL, 1984). See also Rahul Bedi's "Indira Gandhi's Death Remembered," available at news.bbc.co.uk/2/hi/south_asia/8306420.stm. Accessed January 30, 2010.

5. Prime Minister Stephen Harper's Air India memorial speech, www.ctvbc.ctv.ca/servlet/an/local/CTVNews/20100623/harper-text-100623/20100623?hub=BritishColumbiaHome. Accessed January 31, 2010.

6. "A Voyage to Freedom—1948," available at walnut1948.cwahi.net/. Accessed January 30, 2010.

7. Ramdeo Sampat-Mehta, *International Barriers* (Ottawa: Harpell's Press,1973), p. 320.

8. "Landed Immigrant Policy Suspended," front page, *Globe and Mail*, November 4, 1972.

9. "Repair Crew At Work," editorial, *Globe and Mail*, November 4, 1972.

10. Armine Yalnizyan, "Temporary Foreign Workers vs. Economic Immigrants," *Globe and Mail*, February 18, 2011.

11. Audrey Macklin, "The Other Indian Other," in *Storied Communities: Narratives of Contact and Arrival in Constituting Political Community*, eds. H. Lessard, R. Johnson and J. Webber (Vancouver: UBC Press, 2010), p. 60.

12. I was struck by the similarities between what happened with the *Komagata Maru* and in the contemporary history of dealing with refugees while listening

to a lecture by Alison Mountz, author of *Seeking Asylum: Human Smuggling and Bureaucracy at the Border* (Minneapolis, MN: University of Minneapolis Press, 2010), at York University in 2010.

13. Audrey Macklin and Sean Rehaag, "Playing Politics with Refugees," *Toronto Star,* December 3, 2010.

1 | MIGRATIONS AND THE MYTH OF EMPIRE

1. Tony McClenaghan, BEM, JP, General Secretary of the Indian Military Historical Society, was instrumental in helping me narrow down which British military units might have passed through Canada for the Diamond Jubilee celebrations. His colleague Cliff Parrett identified the turbaned Chinese in the 1902 photograph as soldiers belonging to a short-lived, China-based unit, the First Chinese Regiment of the British Army.
2. Sandeep Brar, who created SikhMuseum. com, generously shared this finding with me.
3. Quoted from "Our Lady of the Snows" in Denis Judd's *Empire: The British Imperial Experience from 1765 to the Present* (London: HarperCollins, 1996), pp. 217–218.
4. Hugh Tinker, *A New System of Slavery: The Export of Indian Labour Overseas 1830–1920* (London: Oxford University Press, 1974).
5. Lizzie Collingham, *Curry: A Tale of Cooks and Conquerors* (New York: Oxford University Press, 2006), p. 245.
6. Sir William Muir, ed., "Memorandum, drawn up at the request of the Governor-General, of Enquiries into the alleged dishonour of European females at the time of the mutinies—submitted December 30, 1857," *Records of the Intelligence Department of the Government of the North-West Provinces of India During the Mutiny of 1857*, vol. I (Edinburgh, 1902), pp. 367–79.
7. Christopher Herbert, *War of No Pity: The Indian Mutiny and Victorian Trauma*

(Princeton, NJ: Princeton University Press, 2007), p. 55.
8. Quoted in "The Mechanism of Indian Rule" by Kate Mitchell, in *The British in India: Imperialism or Trusteeship?*, ed. Martin D. Lewis (Boston: Heath, 1962).
9. The Natal Dictation Test emulated one proposed in the United States, in the Immigration Restriction Act of 1896, which was vetoed by President Grover Cleveland. The act would have required immigrants to be literate in their own language. Joseph Chamberlain was inspired by this means of exclusion. Author Marilyn Lake has argued that the origins of the test lie in the Education Test of 1890, which was used in Mississippi to disenfranchise the majority of African American voters.
10. Philip G. Jones and Anna Kenny. *Australia's Muslim Cameleers: Pioneers of the Inland, 1860s–1930s* (Adelaide: Wakefield Press/ South Australia Museum, 2007).
11. Urban geographer Brent Ingram, Vancouver born and raised, made me aware of Vancouver's social geography when I interviewed him for the film *Rex vs. Singh* (2008).
12. *Daily Province*, Vancouver, October 26, 1907.
13. Thos. F. McGuigan to R.W. Scott, Immigration Branch files (RG76, vol. 384, file 536899, pt. I), Library and Archives Canada.
14. Fred Lockley, "The Hindu Invasion," *Pacific Monthly*, vol. XVII, January–June 1907, p. 592.
15. James Pennington MacPherson, *Life of the Right Hon. Sir John A. Macdonald* (Saint John, NB: Earle Publishing, 1891), p. 338.

2 | BUILDING CANADA AS A "WHITE MAN'S COUNTRY"

1. Audrey Macklin, "The Legal History of Canadian Immigration" (unpublished manuscript), p. 11.
2. House of Commons, *Debates* (Hansard), April 30, 1883, p. 114.
3. "A Chronology Focusing on Refugees and Discrimination," Canadian Council for

Refugees website, www.ccrweb.ca/history.
html. Accessed February 10, 2011.

4. I discovered this story in the online
archives of the *New York Times,* attributed
to December 19, 1915; however there are
several facts in it, such as the $25 landing
fee and the relatively unfettered arrival of
South Asians, that indicate the article was
written and likely published before 1908.
Archives at www.nytimes.com accessed
January 1, 2011.

5. A.J. Monroe to W.D. Scott, Immigration
Branch files (R6-72, file 536999, pt. 1),
Library and Archives Canada.

6. Stevenson to Secretary of State, November
19, 1906, Immigration Branch files (R6-72,
file 536999, pt. 1), Library and Archives
Canada.

7. MacPherson to Laurier, September 21,
1906, Immigration Branch files (R6-72,
file 536999, pt. 1), Library and Archives
Canada.

8. David E. Omissi, *The Sepoy and the Raj*
(London: Palgrave Macmillan, 1995), p. 20.

9. Instituted to ensure a disciplined lifestyle
and boldly proclaim Sikh identity, the Five
K's are unshorn hair, a wooden comb, an
iron bracelet, a ceremonial dagger and a
specific undergarment.

10. The commemorative plaque referring to
the soldiers reads "…fighting against
overwhelming numbers, thus proving their
loyalty and devotion to their sovereign, the
Queen Empress of India, and gloriously
maintaining the reputation of the Sikhs for
unflinching courage on the field of battle."
Sikh Courier International, vols. 43–48,
Sikh Cultural Society of Great Britain,
2002, p. 35.

11. Ramdeo Sampat-Mehta, *International
Barriers* (Ottawa: Harpell's Press, 1973),
p. 51.

12. Howard Hiroshi Sugimoto, *Japanese Immigration, the Vancouver Riots, and Canadian
Diplomacy* (New York: Arno Press, 1978),
p. 181.

13. Ted Ferguson, *A White Man's Country:
An Exercise in Canadian Prejudice,*
1st ed. (Garden City, NY: Doubleday, 1975),
p. 30.

14. "Vancouver to Ship Hindus to Ottawa,"
New York Times, September 13, 1907.

15. W.L.M. King, "Report by W.L. Mackenzie King, C.M.G., Deputy Minister of
Labour, on Mission to England to Confer
with British Authorities of the Subject of
Immigration to Canada from the Orient
and Immigration from India in Particular,"
Sessional Papers, 1908, no. 36a, Library
and Archives Canada.

16. Hugh Johnston, *The Voyage of the
Komagata Maru: The Sikh Challenge to
Canada's Colour Bar* (Vancouver: UBC Press,
1989), p. 142.

17. W.L.M. King, "Report on Mission to
England," *Sessional Papers, 1908,* no. 36a,
Library and Archives Canada.

18. House of Commons, *Debates* (Hansard),
1908, p. 6435.

19. W.D. Scott to P. Doyle, Dominion Immigration Agent, Quebec, March 28, 1908.
Quoted in Ramdeo Sampat-Mehta's *International Barriers* (Ottawa: Harpell's Press,
1973), p. 140.

20. According to a Citizenship and Immigration
Canada monograph entitled *Forging our
Legacy* (2000), in 1910, "the average annual
income of a production worker in Canada
was about $417." www.cic.gc.ca/english/
resources/publications/legacy/chap-3.
asp#chap3-3. Accessed February 16, 2011.

21. Khushwant Singh and Satindra Singh,
*Ghadar, 1915: India's First Armed Revolu-
tion* (New Delhi: R & K Publishing House,
1966), p. 8.

22. Letter to a Mr. Walker of Toronto, outlining
the history of South Asian immigration,
April 23, 1915, Immigration Branch files
(RG76, 879545, vol. 602, pt. 6), Library and
Archives Canada.

23. House of Commons, *Debates* (Hansard),
1908, p. 6435.

24. House of Commons, *Debates* (Hansard), 1908, p. 6457.

25. E.J.E. Swayne, "Confidential Memorandum in Matters Affecting the East Indian Community in British Columbia by Colonel E.J.E. Swayne," encl. 3 in no. 2, p. 3, National Archives of India.

26. Swayne also suggested that the government of India introduce passports in order to control those who wished to leave its shores. Few Indians would have guessed their passports came about as a result of the community in North America.

27. Kesar Singh, *Canadian Sikhs (Part One) and the Komagata Maru Massacre,* 2nd ed. (Surrey, BC: Kesar Singh, 1997), p. 22.

28. I have used the term common to that period, the Great Uprising; it is also referred to as India's First War of Independence, the Great Rebellion, the Revolt of 1857, the Uprising of 1857, the Sepoy Rebellion and the Sepoy Mutiny.

29. MacGill to Cory, October 28, 1910, Home Department, Political–A Proceedings, encl. 1 in no. 78, National Archives of India.

30. Hopkinson to W.W. Cory, March 26, 1912, London, U.K., IOLR, JPDP (file 6/1064). Quoted in "The Origins of Political Policing in Canada: Class, Law, and the Burden of Empire" by Andrew Parnaby and Gregory S. Kealey, *Osgoode Hall Law Journal* vol. 41, nos. 2 and 3.

31. "A Revolution in the Making in Vancouver," *New York Times,* June 5, 1910.

32. Audrey Macklin, "The Legal History of Canadian Immigration" (unpublished manuscript), p. 55.

33. Valerie Knowles, *Strangers at Our Gates: Canadian Immigration Policy, 1540–2006* (Toronto: Dundurn Press, 2007), p. 110.

34. Kesar Singh, *Canadian Sikhs (Part One) and the Komagata Maru Massacre,* 2nd ed. (Surrey, BC: Kesar Singh, 1997), p. 93.

35. Kesar Singh, *Canadian Sikhs (Part One) and the Komagata Maru Massacre,* 2nd ed. (Surrey, BC: Kesar Singh, 1997), p. 81.

36. Citizenship and Immigration Canada, "Facts and Figures 2009—Immigration Overview: Permanent and Temporary Residents," www.cic.gc.ca/english/resources/statistics/facts2009/permanent/index.asp. Accessed December 30, 2010.

37. *Daily Province,* Vancouver, October 23, 1913.

38. Audrey Macklin, "The Legal History of Canadian Immigration" (unpublished manuscript), p. 155.

39. *Daily Province,* Vancouver, December 9, 1913.

3 | THE *KOMAGATA MARU* AT THE GATES OF CANADA

1. I have come to know Gurdit Singh not just through archival records and photographs, but also through his own account of the journey, which was self-published years after the voyage. *The Voyage of the Komagata Maru, or India's Slavery Abroad* is an attempt to set the record straight. Gurdit's account often contradicts the official version of events, yet he is careful about his intent. His memoir was published in the late 1920s, when political agitation against the British was growing by the day and being met with increasing repression. Flawed and filled with self-justification as his account might be, it offers personal insight into the motives behind this momentous voyage.

2. Home Department, Political–A Proceedings, November 1914, nos. 97–177, National Archives of India.

3. From the translation of Gurdit Singh's flyer for the journey.

4. Baba Gurdit Singh, *Voyage of the Komagata Maru, or India's Slavery Abroad* (Calcutta: Gurdit Singh, 1928), p. 41.

5. Baba Gurdit Singh, *Voyage of the Komagata Maru, or India's Slavery Abroad* (Calcutta: Gurdit Singh, 1928), pp. 19–21.

6. "The *Komagata Maru* Committee Report," in Home Department, Political–A Proceedings, November 1914, nos. 97–177, National Archives of India.

7. *Japan Advertiser,* Tokyo, April 29, 1914, Immigration Branch files (RG76, vol. 388,

file 536999, pt. 2), Library and Archives Canada.

8. *Daily Province*, Vancouver, April 18, 1914.

9. David Lethbridge, "Canada: Racist Convention Shut Down," *Guardian*, October 20, 1999, at www.sullivan-county.com/news/bicanada.html. Accessed January 30, 2010.

10. Pascoe Goard to H.H. Stevens, April 18, 1914, Immigration Branch files (RG76, vol. 601, file 879545, pt. 1), Library and Archives Canada.

11. H.L. Good to Reid, May 24, 1914, Immigration Branch files (RG76, vol. 601, file 879545, pt. 1), Library and Archives Canada.

12. *Victoria Times*, May 22, 1914.

13. Gurdit Singh to Reid, May 24, 1914, Immigration Branch files (RG76, vol. 601, file 879545, pt. 1), Library and Archives Canada.

14. Reid to Scott, telegram, May 25, 1914, Immigration Branch files (RG76, vol. 601, file 879545, pt. 1), Library and Archives Canada.

15. Reid to Scott, May 26, 1914, Immigration Branch files (RG76, vol. 601, file 879545, pt. 1), Library and Archives Canada.

16. Scott to Reid, telegram, May 26, 1914, Immigration Branch files (RG76, vol. 601, file 879545, pt. 1), Library and Archives Canada.

17. *Daily Province*, Vancouver, May 27, 1914.

18. Hopkinson to Cory, May 31, 1914, Immigration Branch files (RG76, vol. 388, file 536999, pt. 1), Library and Archives Canada.

19. Gurdit Singh, "Shipload of My People," *Victoria Times*, May 22, 1914.

20. House of Commons, *Debates* (Hansard), 1914, p. 4563.

21. Husain Rahim, in the *Hindustanee*, June 1914.

22. Edward Bird, in the *Hindustanee*, June 1914.

23. Scott to Reid, June 5, 1914, Immigration Branch files (RG76, vol. 601, file 879545, pt. 2), Library and Archives Canada.

24. House of Commons, *Debates* (Hansard), June 8, 1914, p. 5027.

25. House of Commons, *Debates* (Hansard), June 10, 1914, p. 5213.

26. House of Commons, *Debates* (Hansard), June 10, 1914.

27. Transcribed from *The Komagata Maru Affair*, a CBC radio documentary produced for the series *Venture*, 1964.

28. Hopkinson to W.W. Cory, June 21, 1914, Immigration Branch files (RG76, vol. 601, file 879545, pt. 2), Library and Archives Canada.

29. Minutes of a Hindu Mass Meeting held in the Dominion Hall, Vancouver, June 21, 1914, Borden Papers, C196(2), vol. 40.

30. Minutes of Public Meeting, Vancouver, June 23, 1914. Borden Papers, C196(2), vol. 40.

31. Bird to Borden, June 23, 1914, Immigration Branch files (RG76, vol. 601, file 879545, pt. 2), Library and Archives Canada.

32. Reid to Scott, June 23, 1914, Immigration Branch files (RG76, vol. 601, file 879545, pt. 2), Library and Archives Canada.

33. Borden to Bird, June 25, 1914, Immigration Branch files (RG76, vol. 601, file 879545, pt. 2), Library and Archives Canada.

34. *Sunset*, Vancouver, June 27, 1914, Immigration Branch files (RG76, vol. 388, file 536999, pt. 2), Library and Archives Canada.

35. Passengers of the *Komagata Maru* to Reid, June 26, 1914, Immigration Branch files (RG76, vol. 601, file 879545, pt. 2), Library and Archives Canada.

36. Hopkinson to Wallinger, June 10, 1914, Immigration Branch files (RG76, vol. 601, file 879545, pt. 2), Library and Archives Canada.

37. Baba Gurdit Singh, *Voyage of the Komagata Maru, or India's Slavery Abroad* (Calcutta: Gurdit Singh, 1928), p. 72.

38. Hugh Johnston, *The Voyage of the Komagata Maru: The Sikh Challenges to Canada's Colour Bar* (Vancouver: UBC Press, 1989), p. 60.

39. Vijay Agnew, *Interrogating Race and Racism* (Toronto: University of Toronto Press, 2007), p. 97.

40. *Gazette*, Montreal, July 8, 1914.

41. Quoted in the *Gazette*, Montreal, July 9, 1914.

42. Bird to Reid, July 9, 1914, Immigration Branch files (RG76, vol. 601, file 879545, pt. 4), Library and Archives Canada.

43. Unpublished memoirs of J. Edward Bird, written in 1940 in Vancouver, p. 93. His grandson Richard Bird, Q.C., generously gave me a copy.

44. Baba Gurdit Singh, *Voyage of the Komagata Maru, or India's Slavery Abroad* (Calcutta: Gurdit Singh, 1928), p. 73.

45. Baba Gurdit Singh, *Voyage of the Komagata Maru, or India's Slavery Abroad* (Calcutta: Gurdit Singh, 1928), p. 73.

46. Hopkinson to Wallinger, July 20, 1914, Immigration Branch files (RG76, vol. 601, file 879545, pt. 4), Library and Archives Canada.

47. Transcribed from *The Komagata Maru Affair*, a CBC radio documentary produced for the series *Venture*, 1964.

48. Hopkinson to Wallinger, July 20, 1914.

49. Stevens to Borden, telegram, July 22, 1914, Borden Papers, C196(2), vol. 40, p. 17729; Immigration Branch files (RG76, vol. 601, file 879545, pt. 4), Library and Archives Canada.

50. Letter from Deputy Minister to Mr. Walker, Esq., April 15, 1915, Immigration Branch files (RG76, vol. 602, file 879545, pt. 6), Library and Archives Canada.

51. Hardinge to Borden, July 19, 1914, Borden Papers, C196(2), vol. 40.

52. Borden to Burrell, July 20, 1914, Immigration Branch files (RG76, vol. 601, file 879545, pt. 4), Library and Archives Canada.

53. Blake Robertson to Reid, July 22, 1914, Immigration Branch files (RG76, vol. 602, file 879545, pt. 5), Library and Archives Canada.

54. Reid to Robertson, July 22, 1914, Borden Papers, C196(2), vol. 40, p. 17701; Immigration Branch files (RG76, vol. 602, 879545, pt. 5), Library and Archives Canada.

55. Baba Gurdit Singh, *Voyage of the Komagata Maru, or India's Slavery Abroad* (Calcutta: Gurdit Singh, 1928), p. 108.

56. Borden to Governor General, July 21, 1914,

Home Department, Political-A Proceedings, November 1914, nos. 97–177, p. 155, National Archives of India.

57. Burrell to Borden, July 22, 1914, Borden Papers, C196(2), vol. 40.

58. Burrell to Borden, July 25, 1914, Borden Papers, C196(2), vol. 40.

59. Burrell to Borden, July 25, 1914, Borden Papers, C196(2), vol. 40, p. 17798.

60. Reid to Scott, July 22, 1914, Immigration Branch files (RG76, vol. 601, file 879545, pt. 4), Library and Archives Canada.

61. Transcribed from *The Komagata Maru Affair*, a CBC radio documentary produced for the series *Venture*, 1964.

EPILOGUE

1. Sandeep Brar, who runs SikhMuseum.com, has researched the life of Buckam Singh, one of eight Sikhs who fought for Canada in the First World War.

2. Translated from a poem recited by Jack Uppal and quoted in my documentary film *Continuous Journey*. Uppal had learned the poem from the book *Ghadar di Goonj*. Translated by Vancouver based writer/poet, Sadhu Binning, 2003.

3. Baba Gurdit Singh, *Voyage of the Komagata Maru, or India's Slavery Abroad* (Calcutta: Gurdit Singh, 1928), p. 49.

4. Home Department, Political-A Proceedings, November 1914, p. 113, National Archives of India.

5. Home Department, Political-A Proceedings, October 1914, no. 1, National Archives of India.

6. Official report of a debate in the Canadian House of Commons on Asiatic immigration. Quoted in "Race, Nationality, Mobility: A History of the Passport" by Radhika Mongia, *Public Culture* vol. 11, no. 3, 1999, p. 550.

7. Balwant Singh's execution was reported in the *Daily News-Advertiser*, Vancouver, February 7, 1917.

8. Singh, Baba Gurdit, *Voyage of the Komagata Maru, or India's Slavery Abroad* (Calcutta: Gurdit Singh, 1928).

SOURCES

OFFICIAL DOCUMENTS AND PARLIAMENTARY PAPERS

Borden Papers, c196(2), vol. 40 (microfilm reel c4232), Library and Archives Canada

House of Commons, *Debates* (Hansard), Canada

Home Department, Political–A Proceedings, November 1914, nos. 97–177, National Archives of India

Immigration Branch Files, RG76-I-A-I, 2, 3 (microfilm reels c10669, c10670, c10280, c10279), Library and Archives Canada

PHOTOGRAPHIC RESEARCH

Alkazi Collection of Photography, New Delhi, India

Bancroft Library, University of California, Berkeley, U.S.

British Columbia Archives, Victoria, Canada

City of Vancouver Archives, Vancouver, Canada

Desh Bhagat Yadgar Hall, Jalandhar, India

Deutsches Schiffahartsmuseum, Bremerhaven, Germany

Kashi House, London, U.K.

Library and Archives Canada, Ottawa, Canada

National Archives of Australia, Canberra, Australia

National Army Museum, London, U.K.

Pardeep Singh Nagra Collection, Toronto, Canada

Peter Walton Collection, U.K.

Power House Museum, Sydney, Australia

Rana Chhina Collection, New Delhi, India

SikhMuseum.com Collection, Mississauga, Canada

Simon Fraser University Library—Special Collections, Burnaby, Canada

State Library of South Australia, Adelaide, Australia

University of Washington Libraries—Special Collections, Seattle, U.S.

Vancouver Public Library—Special Collections, Vancouver, Canada

Washington State Historical Society, Tacoma, U.S.

SELECTED BIBLIOGRAPHY

Dua, Ena. "The Nation and Family: Excluding Indian Female Migrants from Canada," *Canadian Women's Studies*, Fall 2000.

Ferguson, Ted. *A White Man's Country: An Exercise in Canadian Prejudice* (Toronto: Doubleday Canada, 1975).

Johnston, Hugh. "The Surveillance of Indian Nationalists in North America, 1908–1918," *B.C. Studies*, vol. 78, 1988, pp. 3–27.

Johnston, Hugh J.M. *The Voyage of the Komagata Maru: The Sikh Challenge to Canada's Colour Bar* (Delhi: Oxford University Press, 1979).

Josh, Sohan Singh. *Tragedy of the Komagata Maru* (New Delhi: People's Publishing House, 1975).

Macklin, Audrey. "The Other Indian Other," in *Storied Communities: Narratives of Contact and Arrival in Constituting Political Community*, eds. H. Lessard, R. Johnson and J. Webber (Vancouver: UBC Press, 2010).

Mongia, Radhika. "Race, Nationality, Mobility: A History of the Passport," in *After the Imperial Turn: Thinking through Nation*, ed. Antoinette M. Burton (Durham, NC: Duke University Press, 2003), pp. 196–214.

Mountz, Aliso. *Seeking Asylum: Human Smuggling and Bureaucracy at the Border* (Minneapolis, MN: University of Minnesota Press, 2010).

Reid, Robie L. "The Inside Story of the *Komagata Maru*," in *British Columbia Historical Quarterly*, vol. v, no. 1, January 1941, p. 4.

Singh, Baba Gurdit. *Voyage of the Komagata Maru, or India's Slavery Abroad* (Calcutta: Gurdit Singh, 1928).

Singh, Kesar. *Canadian Sikhs (Part One) and the Komagata Maru Massacre*, 2nd ed. (Surrey, BC: Kesar Singh, 1997).

Walker, Barrington, ed. *The History of Immigration and Racism in Canada: Essential Readings* (Toronto: Canadian Scholars' Press, 2008).

Ward, W. Peter. "The *Komagata Maru* Incident," in *White Canada Forever: Popular Attitudes and Public Policy Toward Orientals in British Columbia*, 2nd ed. (Montreal: McGill-Queen's University Press, 1990), pp. 79–93.

PHOTOGRAPHIC CREDITS

All images courtesy of the author except as follows:

p. ii: Rana Chhina Collection (RCC), New Delhi, India

p. iii: RCC, New Delhi, India

p. iv: Canada Dept. of Mines and Resources, Library and Archives Canada (LAC), c-009660, Ottawa, Canada

p. v: LAC, c-7529, photographer: H.H. Stevens, Ottawa, Canada

p. vi: LAC, c-75260, Ottawa, Canada

p. vii: LAC, c-09665, Ottawa, Canada

p. xiv: © 2004 Peripheral Visions Film & Video Inc.

p. xvi: Kartar Singh fonds, LAC, R2094-0-3-E, Ottawa, Canada

p. xvii: Vancouver Public Library (VPL)—Special Collections, VPL 6230, Vancouver, Canada

p. 10: Courtesy of the United Service Institution of India, New Delhi, India

p. 12: Peter Walton Collection (PWC), U.K.

p. 14: *above:* PWC, U.K; right: PWC, U.K; *far right:* PWC, U.K.

p. 20: *right:* Courtesy of the United Service Institution of India, New Delhi, India

p. 20: *below:* National Army Museum, London, U.K., negative number 1198

p. 21: Photograph by Felice Beato, Lucknow Albumen print, 1857–58, 194 × 133 mm, AACP: 99:07:0001(04), Alkazi Collection of Photography, New Delhi, India

p. 22: National Army Museum, London, U.K., negative number 46384

p. 23: National Army Museum, London, U.K., negative number 17356

p. 24: Gurmit Singh and Satnam Singh Collection, Toronto, Canada

p. 25: *left:* Pardeep Singh Nagra Collection, Toronto, Canada

p. 26: *right:* Kashi House, London, U.K; *below:* Courtesy of the United Service Institution of India, New Delhi, India

p. 29: Power House Museum, Sydney, 2007/210/1 Badge, "White Australia Policy," copper-nickel/ aluminum, maker unknown [Sydney, New South Wales, Australia/Melbourne, Victoria, Australia], c. 1920

p. 30: Item number в68916, State Library of South Australia, Adelaide, Australia

p. 31: *left:* Item к1145, 1913/78, National Archives of Australia, Canberra, Australia

p. 32: *above: The Old Waterfront, Vancouver 1898,* painting by John Horton, 1991, courtesy of the artist; *right:* City of Vancouver Archives (cva), мi p2, Vancouver, Canada

p. 33: Philip Timms photograph, vpl, vpl 3027, Vancouver, Canada

p. 34: Vancouver Maritime Museum, Vancouver, Canada

p. 36: University of Washington Libraries—Special Collections, uw 18745, Seattle, U.S.

p. 37: *left:* University of Washington Libraries—Special Collections, uw 15673, Seattle, U.S.

p. 39: cva, Port p1551, Vancouver, Canada

p. 40: Philip Timms photograph, vpl, vpl 7642, Vancouver, Canada

p. 42: vpl—Special Collections, vpl 6227, Vancouver, Canada

p. 44: *above:* lac, pa-010263, Ottawa, Canada; *right:* lac, c-095320, Ottawa, Canada

p. 45: lac, pa-124866, Ottawa, Canada

p. 46: German Maritime Museum (Deutsches schiffahartsmuseum), Bremerhaven, Germany

p. 47: *left:* vpl—Special Collections, vpl 12866, Vancouver, Canada; *below:* lac, c-072064, Ottawa, Canada

p. 48: *top:* vpl—Special Collections, vpl 1773, Vancouver, Canada; *bottom:* © Government of Canada. Reproduced with the permission of the Minister of Public Works and Government Services Canada (2011); Source: lac/Yee Yee Tam fonds/e008441645

p. 50: *below:* F. Douglas Todd photograph, vpl, vpl 2113, Vancouver, Canada

p. 51: *bottom:* vpl—Special Collections, vpl 8118, Vancouver, Canada

p. 55: *left:* Kesar Singh Collection, Canada; *right:* Desh Bhagat Yadgar Hall, Jalandhar, India

p. 57: Pardeep Singh Nagra Collection, Toronto, Canada

p. 58: *above: Collier's Magazine,* September 28, 1907; Source: Asian American Curriculum and Research Project, Western Washington University, Bellingham, U.S.; *right: World's Work* xv (March 1908), F.G. Moorehead, "The Foreign Invasion of the Northwest"; Source: Asian American Curriculum and Research Project, Western Washington University, Bellingham, U.S.

p. 59: *left:* Correspondence, lac, Microfilm Reel c-852, Vol. 477, Pages 128806–128812, Ref мg26-g, Ottawa, Canada; *above: Daily Province,* September 13, 1907, courtesy of the *Vancouver Province*; Source: vpl

p. 60: George Barrowclough photograph, vpl, vpl 9426, Vancouver, Canada

p. 61: lac, pa-25970, Ottawa, Canada

p. 62: Assessment of damages, from *Royal Commission to investigate into the losses sustained by Japanese population of Vancouver, B.C., 1907 (2),* © Government of Canada. Reproduced with the permission of the Minister of Public Works and Government Services Canada (2011); Source: lac, King Papers, file 220, file ref. мg26-j4, page c-33100, photographed by the author, Ottawa, Canada

p. 63: *top:* Photo of damaged Japanese storefront, from *Royal Commission to investigate into losses sustained by the Japanese population of Vancouver, B.C., 1907 (2),* © Government of Canada. Reproduced with the permission of the Minister of Public Works and Government Services Canada (2011); Source: lac, King Papers, file 220, file ref. мg26-j4, page c-33121, Ottawa, Canada; *bottom:* Photo of damaged Japanese storefront, from *Royal Commission to investigate into losses sustained by the Japanese population of Vancouver, B.C., 1907 (2),* © Government of Canada. Reproduced with the permission of the Minister of Public Works and Government Services Canada (2011); Source: lac, King Papers, file 220, file ref. мg26-j4, page c-33142, Ottawa, Canada

p. 64: *right:* Photo of damaged Japanese storefront, from *Royal Commission to investigate into losses sustained by the Japanese population of Vancouver, B.C., 1907 (2)*, © Government of Canada. Reproduced with the permission of the Minister of Public Works and Government Services Canada (2011); Source: LAC, King Papers, file 220, file ref. MG26-J4, page C-33089, Ottawa, Canada; *below:* VPL—Special Collections, VPL 940, Vancouver, Canada

p. 65: *above:* LAC, C-003176, Ottawa, Canada; *left:* © Government of Canada. Reproduced with the permission of the Minister of Public Works and Government Services Canada (2011); Source: LAC/Immigration fonds, Series I-A-I, Volume 384, Part 4, File 536999, Reel C-10280

p. 67: *Report on mission to England to confer with the British authorities on the subject of immigration to Canada from the Orient and immigration from India in particular.* King, William Lyon Mackenzie, 18740950, Ottawa: King's Printer, 1908. 10 p.; 25 cm., P. 5. NLC-11402

p. 68: © Government of Canada. Reproduced with the permission of the Minister of Public Works and Government Services Canada (2011); Source: LAC/Privy Council Office fonds/ Series A-I-A, Volume 952, OIC 1908-1255, page 1, Ottawa, Canada

p. 69: © Government of Canada. Reproduced with the permission of the Minister of Public Works and Government Services Canada (2011); Source: LAC/Privy Council Office fonds/ Series A-I-A, Volume 952, OIC 1908-1255, page 2, Ottawa, Canada

p. 71: *top:* CVA, In P3, Vancouver, Canada; *bottom:* Ralph Hill photograph, SWDM 7-4-27, Saskatoon Western Development Museum, Saskatoon, Canada

p. 73: LAC, C-056088, Ottawa, Canada

p. 74: *above:* LAC, PA-123708, Ottawa, Canada; *right:* Kohaly Collection, Simon Fraser University (SFU) Library—Special Collections, Burnaby, Canada

p. 75: Kohaly Collection, SFU Library—Special Collections, Burnaby, Canada

p. 76: *above:* CVA, Out P1067, Vancouver, Canada; *right:* Philip Timms photograph, VPL, VPL 6781, Vancouver, Canada

p. 77: *left:* CVA, CVA 660348, Vancouver, Canada; *below:* Kohaly Collection, SFU Library—Special Collections, Burnaby, Canada

p. 78: Philip Timms photograph, VPL, VPL 5236, Vancouver, Canada

p. 79: Philip Timms photograph, VPL, VPL 7641, Vancouver, Canada

p. 80: *right:* RCC, New Delhi, India; *far right:* RCC, New Delhi, India

p. 81: RCC, New Delhi, India

p. 82: RCC, New Delhi, India

p. 83: Desh Bhagat Yadgar Hall, Jalandhar, India

p. 84: VPL—Special Collections, VPL 4723, Vancouver, Canada

p. 86: VPL—Special Collections, VPL 6227, Vancouver, Canada

p. 88: Bancroft Library, University of California, Berkeley, U.S.

p. 89: *above:* Washington State Historical Society, photographer: Asahel Curtis, negative number 27254, Tacoma, U.S.; *left:* Washington State Historical Society, photographer: Asahel Curtis, negative number 27255, Tacoma, U.S.

p. 90: Kohaly Collection, SFU Library—Special Collections, Burnaby, Canada

p. 91: *left:* Kohaly Collection, SFU Library—Special Collections, Burnaby, Canada; 91, *above:* Courtesy of John Bird, Toronto, Canada

p. 92: VPL—Special Collections, VPL 136, Vancouver, Canada

p. 94: Desh Bhagat Yadgar Hall, Jalandhar, India

p. 95: Kohaly Collection, SFU Library—Special Collections, Burnaby, Canada

p. 96: CVA, CVA 7-128, Vancouver, Canada

p. 98: *Vancouver Sun*, May 24, 1914, courtesy of the *Vancouver Sun*

p. 99: VPL—Special Collections, VPL 136, Vancouver, Canada

p. 100: *top:* VPL—Special Collections, VPL 133, Vancouver, Canada; *bottom:* Leonard Frank photograph, VPL, VPL 6226, Vancouver, Canada

p. 102: Painting by James Hill, published in *Maclean's*, November 8, 1958, reprinted with permission from the Estate of the artist James Hill; Source: Pardeep Singh Nagra Collection, Toronto, Canada

p. 103: *left:* © Government of Canada. Reproduced with the permission of the Minister of Public Works and Government Services Canada (2011); Source: LAC/Immigration fonds, Series 1-A-1, Vol. 601, Part 1, File 879545, Reel C-10669, Ottawa, Canada; *below:* Leonard Frank photograph, VPL, VPL 6231, Vancouver, Canada

p. 104: VPL—Special Collections, VPL 13156, Vancouver, Canada

p. 105: *above:* CVA, CVA 7-126, Vancouver, Canada; *left:* LAC, C-75263, Ottawa, Canada

p. 107: Courtesy of Jack (Jagat) Uppal, Vancouver, Canada

p. 108: *Vancouver Sun*, June 5, 1914, courtesy of the *Vancouver Sun*

p. 109: Courtesy of the Council, National Army Museum, London, U.K.; Source: VPL—Special Collections, VPL 127, Vancouver, Canada

p. 110: © Government of Canada. Reproduced with the permission of the Minister of Public Works and Government Services Canada (2011); Source: LAC/Immigration fonds, Series 1-A-1, Vol. 601, Part 2, File 879545, Item 19063, Reel C-10669, Ottawa, Canada

p. 112: Courtesy of the Council, National Army Museum, London, U.K.; Source: VPL—Special Collections, VPL 122, Vancouver, Canada

p. 113: *Vancouver Sun*, June 5, 1914, courtesy of the *Vancouver Sun*

p. 114: CVA, CVA 141-4, photographer: James L. Quiney, Vancouver, Canada

p. 118: CVA, CVA 141-4, photographer: James L. Quiney, Vancouver, Canada

p. 119: *World*, July 6, 1914; Source: LAC, RG76-A-4, C-10280, B-13746

p. 121: VPL—Special Collections, VPL 129, Vancouver, Canada

p. 122: LAC, PA-034017, Ottawa, Canada

p. 124: *right:* VPL—Special Collections, VPL 6224, Vancouver, Canada; *below:* LAC, PA-034015, Ottawa, Canada

p. 125: LAC, PA-5579, Ottawa, Canada

p. 126: *right:* VPL—Special Collections, VPL 123, Vancouver, Canada; *below:* LAC, PA-034016, Ottawa, Canada

p. 127: VPL—Special Collections, VPL 6223, Vancouver, Canada

p. 128: Leonard Frank photograph, VPL, VPL 6232, Vancouver, Canada

p. 129: *left:* *Vancouver Sun*, June 26, 1914, courtesy of the *Vancouver Sun*; *below:* LAC, C-075262, Ottawa, Canada

p. 130: VPL—Special Collections, VPL 130, Vancouver, Canada

p. 131: VPL—Special Collections, VPL 6229, Vancouver, Canada

p. 134: *below:* Pardeep Singh Nagra Collection, Toronto, Canada

p. 135: SikhMuseum.com, Sandeep Singh Brar Collection, Mississauga, Canada

p. 136: *right:* RCC, New Delhi, India

p. 138: SikhMuseum.com, Sandeep Singh Brar Collection, Mississauga, Canada

p. 139: *below:* LAC, PA-034012, Ottawa, Canada

p. 140: LAC, PA-034011, Ottawa, Canada

p. 141: *left:* Kesar Singh Collection, Canada; *below:* Imperial War Museum, Q 82506, London, U.K.

p. 142: Kohaly Collection, SFU Library—Special Collections, Burnaby, Canada

p. 144: Kohaly Collection, SFU Library—Special Collections, Burnaby, Canada